HIGH BALLS AND
HAPPY HOURS

HIGH BALLS

AND HAPPY HOURS

An Autobiography

GAVIN HASTINGS

WITH CLEM THOMAS

MAINSTREAM
PUBLISHING

EDINBURGH AND LONDON

To the two most important women in my life,
my mother Isobel and my wife Diane

First published in Great Britain in 1994 by
MAINSTREAM PUBLISHING COMPANY (EDINBURGH) LTD
7 Albany Street
Edinburgh EH1 3UG

ISBN 1 85158 645 8

A catalogue record for this book is available from the
British Library

Typeset in Palatino by Pioneer Associates Ltd, Perthshire
Printed in Great Britain by Butler and Tanner Ltd, Frome

Contents

FOREWORD

by
Ian McGeechan OBE

I HAVE been through a lot with Gavin Hastings, from tremendous highs to desperate lows, in a very special eight seasons of rugby, from 1986 to 1993.

My first meeting with him was five years earlier, when I was coaching the Scotland Under-21 team. I remember him as a very chirpy and confident full back, who told me not to worry about where the ball would go, 'It will end up in the right place.' I was not allowed any doubts and so it has proved. Andrew Gavin Hastings has been in the right place on innumerable occasions and I have breathed many great sighs of relief, either watching Scotland or the British Lions.

One of his greatest assets has been to engender confidence in those around him, and to lead by example when the opposition had to be 'taken on', whether it was by standing unflinchingly under a high ball from Grant Fox or Michael Lynagh, or taking the ball on with such strength of purpose from scrums and rucks, as he did against Western Samoa in the 1991 World Cup.

He is a big man in every sense of the word and, just as Kipling wrote, has met squarely with those two impostors, triumph and disaster.

For me, Gavin epitomises the best of International players; he is passionately Scottish but he is also sincerely British, and he has always shown a genuine commitment and endeavour to both roles.

Who could forget the traumas of his first cap (my first game as Assistant Coach) when, with adrenalin flowing, the opening kick-off went straight into touch? Not the best start, but then, having jogged back into the 22 ready for the midfield scrum, he turned to find seven Frenchmen running at him. Needless to say, the odds were in France's favour and, sure enough, a try was scored. So having kicked off, France had scored a try and not one Scottish player had touched the ball! Interestingly, not one Scottish head went down and Gavin, on his debut, duly turned a determined Scottish effort into 18 points with six penalties to win the match 18-17. Murrayfield was alive with tension and excitement and Gavin Hastings had arrived, to become instrumental in developing a unique period of Scottish rugby history.

Whether he was on the practice field or in a match, he was determined to get it right. I remember him finishing a training session in Australia in 1989 kicking high ball after high ball up to the posts, so that he could catch every ball with a solid base and turn his shoulder to take the contact anticipated from the Australian pack in the crucial third Test. On the day, although under intense physical and nervous pressure, he did not drop a ball. When the Lions needed a big man, he had practised to be one. He also kicked the five penalties for a one-point series win.

In New Zealand, they consider him simply the best full back in the world and he has endeared himself not just to them but to fans in every country, because he always had a smile and time for a quick word. He has the ability to put people at ease and make them feel important; in every way he is the true rugby ambassador. I wonder how many youngsters have set their sights on International rugby, not by exploits, but because Gavin let them get close to International rugby through him and his few words? As Lions captain in 1993, every training session invariably concluded with Gavin surrounded by schoolboys and girls wanting his autograph and he did not disappoint any one of them.

His strength as a captain lies in the thoughtfulness he has for his players. On the morning of an International, he would go around the rooms and speak to every player, simply to show how much they matter and that he cares. When tactics dictated that Western Samoa, in the 1991 World Cup, had to be run at so that the big tackles could not come in, it was Gavin who set the standard. I can still picture him coming in on the blind side from scrums and standing outside Gary Armstrong at the rucks, ready to take the ball on and meet the Samoans on his terms. What followed was one of Scotland's most dynamic performances.

We had our lows as well; losing in New Zealand in 1990 and

to England in the semi-final of the 1991 World Cup, but they only served to show how much Scotland and the Lions, with Gavin Hastings, have achieved. If I had to recount to Gavin one incident which shows my admiration for him, it would be the conversation we had on the training field at Wellington the day before the second Test in 1993, when he was doubtful that he could play. I said then, and I still mean and believe it now, that Gavin is so influential concerning the attitudes of others, that his leading the team on to the field, even if it was only for 30 seconds of rugby, would mean the difference between success and defeat. The rest is history.

In the Grand Slam season of 1990, one memory remains clear in my mind, which illustrates the effect that Gavin can have on the flow of a game. It came during the French game at Murrayfield, when France started the second period with a strong wind behind them and followed a first half in which Scotland had spent most of the time in the French half but managed only three points. The French, at the first opportunity, put up a high ball and Gavin collected in front of his posts. He then proceeded to produce the most prodigious kick into the wind, which sent the French back to the halfway. The French backs looked at one another in disbelief and the spring in their step noticeably lessened, as Gavin had taken away a psychological advantage. The match ended as a 21-0 defeat for France.

One of the most disappointing results for us was the 21-18 defeat inflicted on Scotland in the second Test in New Zealand in 1990. Although we lost, this remains for me an outstanding Scottish performance and I am sure it was instrumental in the All Blacks' subsequent defeat by Australia. The game started with Gavin landing two huge penalties from inside his own half, which audibly made the Auckland crowd draw in its breath. There then followed some of the most confident and positive rugby Scotland has ever played. It was Gavin who provided the momentum.

As a coach and 'watcher', Gavin has given me tremendous pleasure and pride. He has been part of a very special period and, at this time of writing, he has just one more team to take forward – Scotland 1995 and the World Cup.

As always, I wish him well.

Ian McGeechan
Edinburgh – August 1994

INTRODUCTION

An Appreciation by Clem Thomas

LYING CLOSE BY the Firth of Forth, and cradled on one side by the snow-capped Pentland Hills, Edinburgh was as cold as charity in early February 1994 when I went to meet three of the grandest and most valorous names in Scottish rugby, Finlay Calder, David Sole and the subject of this book, Gavin Hastings.

Meeting for lunch is always a pleasurable experience, but when three such staunch comrades, who have developed a towering friendship after soldiering together both on and off the rugby field, at home and in foreign parts for the best part of a decade, met at McKenzie's restaurant in the suburbs of Auld Reekie, then it was something special. Alas, the fourth man, Ian McGeechan, who is another you would choose to have in the trenches with you, had called off with the flu.

All four have been honoured by the Queen with the Order of the British Empire for services to rugby, and this was to be Gavin's inaugural OBE lunch, given by Finlay. It seemed to be a pretty solemn affair, that was until Finlay sat down and, with a straight face, said, 'Where's your gong, then?' In some confusion Gavin confessed that he had not yet received it from the Queen, whereupon Finlay promptly flashed back the lapel of his coat to reveal the impressive, red-ribboned gold cross decoration pinned to his shirt. With a straight face he said, 'This is what it is all about.' It took Gavin a few seconds to grasp the joke, but from that moment the restaurant was assailed with laughter and you knew this was going to be one of those great fun lunches that rugby football often provides all over the world. You could see how at home they were in each other's company and that for the rest of their lives there would be that indefinable and unbreakable bond which rugby football seems to forge.

A party of businessmen in a corner of the restaurant had spotted them and, in their reserved Scottish way, allowed them their privacy; but on leaving one of them could not resist saying, 'Is that the Lions' Den?', which of course it was, and they acknowledged the compliment of instant recognition as if it was the most natural thing in the world. High-profile men such as these three are, in their own country and in rugby circles throughout the world, are nevertheless totally unspoilt, modest, highly respected, and terrific people.

This autobiography concerns only one of them, Andrew Gavin Hastings, known as Gav to his friends. To captain one's club, the Watsonians, London Scottish, Cambridge University, the Barbarians, Scotland and the British Lions is the sort of stuff that dreams are made of. If you also command the great respect and affection that the public has lavished on one of rugby's most charismatic characters, then you begin to comprehend the importance of Gavin Hastings. The combination of fine rugby player, automatic choice at full back for two Lions Tours, inspirational captain and one of life's great gentlemen is irresistible.

Born on 3 January 1962 in Edinburgh, to Isobel and Clifford Hastings, Gavin is currently a Marketing Executive with Carnegie Sports International, with offices in London, Edinburgh and New Zealand, where All Black Grant Fox heads the operation. It is part of Murray International Holdings, a conglomerate owned by David Murray, who is also Chairman and major shareholder of Rangers Football Club in Glasgow. One of Gavin's responsibilities is the running of the Super-10 competition in the Southern Hemisphere.

Gavin Hastings is not only one of the great rugby footballers of his era, but he is a person who has brought enormous dignity to the game itself due to his remarkable aura of obvious decency and the capacity to inspire which captivates so many people, whether they know him personally or not.

I have been involved with International rugby for 45 years, for I played for Wales against France in 1949, since which time I have either played with, watched, reported or known virtually all the leading players of the world. Rugby has almost been a way of life for me, my greatest passion, not only because I recognise it as a great game which encapsulates great skills, derring-do and courage, but because I have so much enjoyed those marvellous people who inhabit it.

I am, therefore, well qualified to recognise that Gavin has unusual talents, not only by virtue of his skilful and valiant performances, but because he possesses those indefinable additional qualities which give other people inspiration. If I was asked what was his best attribute, I would say that it was his natural abilities of leadership and authority. All this is combined with a delightful amiability and a gift for pleasing, derived from his good looks and personal charm, and perhaps, above all, a kind nature, which is so refreshing in this day of the anti-hero when a lunatic fringe of the tabloid press can bemoan the absence of tantrums at Wimbledon. Too often the headlines and the sympathy are given to the spoilt brats who, in my view, diminish the sports they represent.

This might seem to be over the top, but my views are vindicated when I remind myself of what his father, Clifford, who is more pragmatically critical of his four sons and the last man in the world to do any bragging, told me when we were discussing Gavin. 'I know it sounds nauseous, but Gavin was always a fine chap with people, with a very nice way about him. It is really difficult to find anything to criticise him for. Once, when we visited Cambridge, we met the bus driver who drove the Varsity team all over England. He would have done anything for Gavin, for he had gone out of his way to be kind to him. I know it all sounds too good to be true, but it seems that, in him, there are all the best ingredients of life.'

The first time Clifford realised that he might have a good player in the family was when the eminent Ken Scotland, who was a founder member of the attacking and running school of full backs, and one in a long line of superlative Scottish full backs, which also included magnificent players like Andy Irvine and Peter Dods, came up to him and said that he had seen Gavin playing at Murrayfield. Ken told him that Gavin had not put a foot wrong. 'When somebody like that says something about your son, then you have to realise that perhaps he has talent. But in a funny sort of way I don't suppose I ever recognised it at the time. At that stage, Gavin and Scott were in the pipeline which took them through the different age levels of school and university, and they were the usual difficult formative years. So much can go wrong at this stage of their lives, and you often find schoolboy caps and "B" Internationals disappear off the face of the earth.'

Clifford believed that Gavin's big breakthrough came when he played for Edinburgh against the New Zealand touring team of 1983, which was his first major game. He made his first impact on the International scene when he came into the final trial in 1986, and helped the Reds beat the Blues by a cricket score. 'That was the beginning of the whole business, and both he and Scott won caps.' Subsequently, Gavin won 13 caps in 1986 and 1987.

Modestly, Clifford believes they were in the right place at the right time, but nevertheless they developed into marvellous players. He recalls three of Gavin's best moments. 'I remember when he scored that astonishing try against France at Murrayfield, when he intercepted a chip ahead, punted on and ran to Berbizier's blind side, where the Frenchmen tried to kick it dead into touch, but Gavin kicked on and touched down. Another time he played for the British Lions against France in Paris, after the 1989 Lions Tour, when he scored an unbelievable try. He cut inside four defenders who tried to crunch him, but, due to his great strength, they all bounced off him, and there was a perilous moment when the last tackler knocked him off balance, and again he used his strength to recover and regain his poise to score a fabulous try.

'On another occasion the British Lions were suffering, as they often do, against the Maoris. They were getting hammered up to half-time, but Ieuan Evans turned the tide by scoring two fine tries to get them back into the game. Three minutes from time Gavin scored a try, when he ignored men outside him and cut in to beat three defenders and, although tackled by the full back some five yards out, he managed to power over the line for the try. These are the three highlights I have in my mind's eye when I look back over Gavin's career.

'He's the sort of chap who is always there, or thereabouts, for that is his nature. People complain that they put the ball down his throat, but, if you watch him, he's always on the move. In much the same way, I have a similar admiration for Scott, for, like Gavin, he is never out of a game of rugby. Whenever he tackles somebody, or is tackled, I have never seen anybody who is quicker to his feet than Scott after putting somebody to grass. That is the great strength of the two brothers; they are always terribly aware of what is going on around them, and I think that has a lot to do with their success.'

Gavin's mother, Isobel, is an avid fan of her boys. Her kitchen wall is a pastiche of press cuttings, and although she loves all her boys equally, she seems to have a particularly soft spot for Gavin.

She told me, 'As brothers, Gavin and Scott were in the middle, so they were left to fend for themselves. Gavin was always the builder, and his elder brother Graeme was the destroyer. If Gavin would build something, Graeme would knock it down, but Gavin would keep on building and he was always more academic than his brothers. There was endless rivalry between the two elder boys and, indeed, between Gavin and Scott, who were always quarrelling over one thing or the other. However, as they grew up, they all came closer together and they are now tremendously close, whereas at one stage I thought they would never be friends, especially the older two. Happily, that has all changed and they now take great pleasure from each other's company.

'People have often asked, "How did you ever encourage them to become so competitive and how did you focus them to become such good players?" I don't think we ever did anything consciously in that regard in any way, except for one thing. One day, Graeme came in and said he could kick the ball the length of the garden and Clifford, my husband, said that he wasn't interested until he came back and said he could do it with both feet. We insisted that they had to be able to kick the ball with the left foot as well as the right, but then they picked that up between themselves, and in this way they helped each other.'

At school, the Hastings brothers were average, but Gavin, the best of them academically, was finally able to get into Cambridge. However, there was no question of applying at the end of his schooling, for at that time he did not possess the necessary qualifications required by Oxbridge. Gavin went to Paisley College of Technology (now Paisley University) and got a BSc in Land Economics, and then went up to Cambridge to read Land Economy, where he got his Masters Degree. He was encouraged to go by Ian Robertson, the BBC's lively rugby correspondent, who was one of the Cambridge coaches at the time. Finally, he got a letter from Mark Bailey, who was first capped on the South African Tour in 1984 and who is now a Fellow at Corpus Christi, a fine amusing man who helped sponsor him with the authorities.

Clifford had to shell out for the two years at Cambridge, but was glad to do so on the principle of supplying according to need, so there was no envy from the rest of the family. Isobel relates, 'We were lucky with the four boys, for there were no real problems apart from the usual horseplay and fighting, and as they got older the stupidities were forgotten. We were left only with happy memories. Although they won their 50th caps at the same time, strangely Scott has seemed to stand one step behind Gavin, for there has always been that natural seniority of the older brother, but then Scott has always been entirely helpful and, when Gavin was made captain of Scotland, it was Scott who was his principal supporter.'

It was Clifford who made the point that, for all his virtues, Gavin was no goody-goody. 'On one occasion, we were all together on a Sunday night as a family and Gavin came and joined us for a meal. There had been a game on the Saturday and he was just a little bit full of himself. He was met by a silence and, an hour later, he said there was a funny atmosphere and asked what was wrong. We just said that we thought he was thoroughly obnoxious and big-headed. He rang up the following day and said, "I have been thinking about what you said and you are right. I was completely out of order and I am sorry." Gavin will tell you that we have rarely praised him for his achievements; more often than not we have criticised him.

'Another time he went across to play for Scotland "B" in Ireland and he met a girl on the Saturday night, after the game, and decided to see her home. He failed to get back to the hotel, or to catch the plane back to Edinburgh for a squad session on the Sunday. He thought that was the end of his career but we got him to write a letter before one came the other way, and happily it was quickly forgotten about.'

Gavin had other interests at Cambridge, apart from rugby. In particular, he had a great admiration for the rowers because of their commitment and stamina. He thought that the oarsmen were tremendous because they had a dedication which he, at the time, as a rugby player simply did not have. He was terribly impressed with the way those people went out at such unsociable hours, in the morning and late at night, to have another hour on the river. He thoroughly enjoyed the bumps and the rowing fraternity and, had he not been so interested in rugby, he might well have got involved in rowing, for he respected them so much. Golf was his other passion and, although he represented the University on a couple of occasions, rugby again got in the way of his aspirations.

Jim Telfer, himself a great player and an extremely strong, blunt personality, who is now the Scottish Coaching Director, is another who has a high opinion of Gavin – 'Gavin Hastings is a really charming bloke, with no side to him at all. One moment he is talking to a rugby man and the next minute he is in conversation with somebody who knows nothing about the game. He has represented Scottish rugby so well wherever he goes, and he is a delightful and articulate man. He has that innate ability of the great player to focus quickly on the job in hand and to be mentally hard. He has been the rock behind the Scottish pack and his forwards knew that, when the ball went behind them, he was a tower of strength and a total redoubt. His presence on the field is immense and he has a terrific effect on the other players. If you had 15 Gavin Hastings you could beat the world.'

Equally, whenever I have discussed Gavin with other great Scots, such as Bill McLaren, the most respected and impeccable voice of rugby, both in Scotland and anywhere in the world, or with Norman Mair, Scotland's most animated rugby writer, they too have confirmed his status as a great player and emphasise the affection that everybody in Scotland seems to have for him.

There have been times, however, when Gavin could be forgiven for believing that somebody up there did not like him, as to lose two of the most crucial matches of his marvellous career within the space of eight months, that first Test in New Zealand during the summer of 1993 and the second, that climactic game against England in the winter of 1994, at the whim of a referee, was an agonizing anguish and enough to make the bravest man cry.

In fact, so upset was Gavin over the loss at Murrayfield that he briefly broke down during the post-match television interview and was taken to task in a newspaper article by my old friend Colin Welland, who is probably Rugby League's greatest single supporter. I must say that I was surprised that a man who had written *Chariots of Fire*, among other fine film scripts, with such sensitivity, should object so vociferously to the dropping of a tear. After all, Eric Elwood, Ireland's new strong man at outside half, admitted to the same offence in the dressing-room after losing the Welsh game in Dublin, and we all saw Gazza wiping a tear from his sad face during a soccer World Cup. I can only surmise that Colin was really feeling and railing against the recent hostile treatment of the English at Murrayfield, which the Scots call a bit of fun, while the English call it jingoistic nationalism.

In the event, the occasion brought Gavin his greatest mail bag ever, as hundreds of letters of sympathy and support poured through his letterbox, from such disparate personalities as a colonel in the Royal Marines, and young and old ladies from the English shires. Somehow he had touched a chord which would not have been reached by a stiff upper lip.

One of the amusing incidents of Gavin's career came during

the recent Lions' tour when the impish Ian Robertson, rugby correspondent and one of life's great wheeler dealers, spotted a group of some 50 Japanese rugby supporters arriving at his hotel in Hamilton, New Zealand. Having been privy to a deal when the Lions bought a job lot of rugby balls, which they autographed and sold at an outrageous profit for the tour fund, Ian quickly grasped the opportunity and asked them whether they would like to meet Gavin Hastings. Their eyes lit up, so Ian said, 'Come with me', and they followed him in a crocodile to the team hotel where a few of the Lions, including Rob Andrew and Brian Moore, stood wide-eyed in astonishment and admiration as Robertson then said, 'Hands up those who want to buy a rugby ball autographed by the Lions for only a hundred dollars?' A few hands went up and Robertson said, 'Come on. No rugby balls, no Gavin Hastings.' Reluctantly, another eight hands went up and Robertson again gently chided them, until finally they all surrendered.

Gathering in the money, Robertson now asked Rob Andrew, 'Where's Gavin?', only to be told he was not in his room. Panic! Finally, he was found in the gym having a shower, where Ian, after telling him about the Japanese waiting to meet him, was politely told to 'flick off'. However, realising the scope of the transaction, Gavin reluctantly allowed himself to be dragged into the hall, where the Japanese walked around him in some wonder. According to Chris Rea, who told me the story, it was an extremely funny scene, as one or two even poked him with a finger as though he was from another planet.

It has been a considerable pleasure assisting and co-operating with Gavin in compiling his autobiography. All I have done is to help marshal the facts and the shape of his book, and to prompt him to remember significant moments and help him to express his beliefs on so many aspects of the game.

Many of his views are extremely radical and will, I believe, give us all food for thought, particularly as to what direction the game is taking and how it can be improved. He also gives us a clear insight into his rugby life and times, and the book celebrates some of Scottish, and British, rugby's finest moments.

If we have made any errors of memory or fact, it was not through lack of effort, but any mistakes will be irrelevant to the many observations and ideas expressed by Gavin in his book, for which both he and I, after careful checking, take joint responsibility.

Clem Thomas
Swansea – August 1994

CHAPTER I

A Radical Proposal

I WAS BORN on 3 January 1962 and started playing rugby football when I was ten years old. My association with the game has been a source of pleasure, fun and excitement, as well as hard work and dedication, and the majority of my book is concerned with that story.

I have observed, and been involved in, enormous changes over that time which make me proud of the potential of this great game as a world sport, but also anxious that we should do everything possible to improve it and make it accessible to a wider and wider audience. In later chapters, I discuss the influences that are shaping the future of the game, but right at the beginning I want to turn attention to what I consider to be a simple proposal that could have an effect on the game out of all proportion to the organisational effort it would require.

Let us make it a summer, not a winter, sport.

The far, far better weather enjoyed by the southern hemisphere countries gives them a huge advantage over us Europeans. You simply cannot compare the winter climates of Australia, New Zealand and South Africa with the sort of hellish weather conditions of the British winter, through which we have to train and play. We often need three or four layers of clothing, including thermals, with waterproof tops over training jerseys and track suits, which makes it very difficult to work up much enthusiasm for training and inhibits our ball skills and freedom of movement.

I therefore put forward my proposal for improving the game,

its attraction to the players and to the public at large in the British Isles, by earnestly and strongly advocating looking at alternative times of the year to play rugby. I believe that our game would improve out of sight and become far better supported if it were transferred to the summer months. In a place like Scotland, in Ireland too, and to a lesser extent Wales, I am sure it would work. In England it would be very much harder because of the influence of cricket, but they would have to learn to live with that, just as, at present, Rugby Union and Rugby League compete with soccer in the winter months.

We could start playing rugby in March and go right through to the end of October. We would then be playing at the same time of the year as the southern hemisphere countries, which would make it far easier to organise World Cups or tours between respective countries. We could all go on tour at the same time of the season, either at the start or at the end, which would not prolong our rugby-playing year unduly, instead of the present system which often sees us playing rugby for close on 12 months of the year. I have no doubt that this one radical change would dramatically improve the quality of British Isles rugby, and, indeed, its popularity.

Why should rugby be a winter game? Surely only because traditionally it always has been seen as capable of being played in bad weather, but I say we should change and adapt in order to give ourselves the best possible opportunity of competing against the finest sides in the world. In Fiji and Samoa they play their rugby in warm, humid conditions, and their ball handling skills are absolutely unbelievable.

The whole game is changing and improving world wide and, unless we are careful, we are going to get left behind, make no mistake about that. For instance, Western Samoa have become a serious power after beating Wales twice within three years and getting to the quarter finals of the 1991 World Cup. It is a small island in the South Pacific with a population of some 170,000, who, like the Irish in America, have spread widely into New Zealand, where they play a major part in the rugby scene and have a significant influence on both Provincial and All Black rugby. Surely, per capita, they are currently the most powerful rugby nation on earth. Much of that is to do with climate and diet, and it helps that they are also a warrior people.

Their winters are often better than our summers and they are running around in shorts and T-shirts doing their training. How

can we be as committed when we are often out in freezing temper-
atures and pouring rain in the middle of the desperate British
winter? It is in everyone's interest to run around and keep fit in
the summer time, but logically only to wrap up and keep warm in
the winter time.

Surely it is up to us to make our climate work to our advantage! I am totally convinced that if rugby people within the UK
were to sit down and analyse what I am saying, then they would
agree that summer rugby is a good idea and imperative for the
future and health of the game in Northern Europe. We can really
make this work. Another important consideration is that you do
not need thousands of rugby pitches, just one pitch on which to
play three or four games would suffice; you could start at midday,
and let the matches roll on while others are organising a barbecue
and a crêche for the kids, and the families can come along and set
out their picnics, the beer in the ice-boxes, and enjoy a lovely day
in the open air. Recently, before England's remarkable win against
the Springboks at Loftus Versfeld in Pretoria, the curtain raiser,
which not only encourages the crowd to get to their seats early but
keeps their interest, was a game involving the Provincial side,
Northern Transvaal. In the United Kingdom you would not
dare risk a curtain raiser before a Test match on any one of our
International pitches because of the probability of bad weather.

Where and in what conditions would people prefer to play
rugby? In Pretoria or Jo'burg, where there is no rain and the
ground is firm, or in Scotland and Wales, where you are freezing
your tail off and slogging your guts out on a dirty, horrible, wet,
cold night, under artificial lights? How can you expect to see
free-flowing rugby and terrific skills exhibited when guys are
waddling around in mud, instead of the short grass and firm
grounds of South Africa and Australia? I believe also that players
perform better on the International stage than for their clubs
because of more detailed preparation and better prepared pitches,
coupled with increased crowd enthusiasm.

In summer time, training would be a pleasure. You would not
need floodlights because of the late summer nights, and the
money saved could go into better preparation and better training
equipment. Rugby balls would not get waterlogged and dirty and
neither would your kit, which would last much longer.

People might say that it would get too hot at certain times of
the year, but then we could play the bigger games at five or six
o'clock in the evening. Most of the time our summer temperature

21

much beyond 20 degrees Centigrade and who says that we have to play at three o'clock in the afternoon? Others suggest that the pitches would get too hard, but there is a commodity called water, which you can use to soften pitches. They use it on golf courses, soccer fields and race courses the world over. It is no harder a task to keep a rugby pitch watered, and I honestly do not think that there are any big problems in the way of summer rugby. We might even get away from competing with soccer, but I expect that would not last very long as they would surely see the benefits and would quickly follow suit! Pitches in Australia and South Africa, and sometimes even in New Zealand, can be very hard indeed, and remember that winter on the high veldt is the dry season, with the ground often so hard that you can hear the drumming of the boots.

It is often said that rugby was designed as a winter game, and people ask, 'What are you going to do without it in the winter?' First of all, I am not sure that a handling game was designed for the wet and cold, and, as for other winter activities, there is plenty to do. We could go skiing, play tennis, basketball or golf, but at least training could be indoors. They also point out that American football is the biggest football game in the world and is often played in hard weather and freezing cold, such as in the Mile High Stadium in Denver. However, they have an incredibly short season of four months, with only 16 regular season games, while the rest of America play in astrodomes or in the balmy, warm atmosphere of Florida, California and other southern states. Our regular season is now over eight months long, and senior players involved in World Cups, Lions Tours and touring with their individual countries, more often than not are playing rugby throughout the whole year.

I know that the Five Nations Championship is a boon to television programmers, for it covers a period of the year when everything else is fairly quiet; but surely it is not beyond their wit, together with that of rugby's administrators, to provide fixtures which do not clash too much – after all, a cricket Test match goes on for five days, whereas we require a mere hour and a half of playing time.

Inevitably, it is going to happen one day, if only for the reason that there are too many sporting climaxes happening in May. You have the end of the three football seasons, with various cup finals, the Grand National, and the start of the cricket, tennis, golf and flat racing seasons, whereas very little happens in September or

October unless there is a major rugby team touring in the United Kingdom.

The four Home Unions are so conservative that I am sure it would take a long time to convince them that my blueprint will give a better and more productive future for British Isles rugby. However, I do believe that if they want to remain at the forefront of world rugby, something radical needs to take place. If they do not reach agreement, which is certainly more likely in the short term, I would like to see the Scottish Rugby Union going it alone.

These days, apart from the Five Nations matches, clubs in Scotland are only playing each other anyway, so there is nothing to stop us from having our own season. There is likely to be a maximum squad of 30 Scottish players involved in the Five Nations preparation, and we could easily get them together into a training camp during that period. We could play these players against each other and take them off for the odd game in France to harden them up. Furthermore, there has been talk of the Five Nations being moved to March or April, by which time the game may have gone totally professional.

I repeat that, in my considered opinion, we will never consistently compete with the southern hemisphere unless we make such a radical change as playing our rugby during the summer months. If the four Home Unions individually want to remain second-rate, then it is up to them, but we, the players, want to compete on equal terms and to have the opportunity to become the world champions in our game.

CHAPTER II

Happy Days

WHENEVER I READ about schools neglecting sporting activity in their curricula and even, in many cases, opting out altogether, I am deeply concerned not only for rugby football but for the whole future of sport in the British Isles. God knows we are doing badly enough in world terms as it is.

So many sports were invented, if that is the correct word, within these shores, that we certainly stole a march on other countries, but it is frightening to me that we now languish way behind in many sports, particularly football and rugby, both in a coaching sense and in the dedication and commitment required from the athletes themselves.

My formative school years were invaluable, not only in igniting my interest in all games, but in keeping me out of mischief. I am the product of many dedicated people, who saw to it that my interest in sport, and in rugby football in particular, was aroused.

I suppose it all began at George Watson's College when, from the age of five, I used to play football in the primary school playground. I remember the school janitor lining us up prior to going into our classrooms in the morning, to give prizes for the cleanest pair of shoes. My Dad used to be very finicky about these things and he would always polish our shoes every morning, so I was lucky. I used to take an old pair of training shoes to change into as soon as I arrived, to play football in, and when we lined up for inspection I quickly got my clean shoes out of my bag, and used to win lots of Mars bars, which aroused some envy in my schoolmates. It was really thanks to my Dad, who taught me at an early age the value of being well turned out.

These were formative times and we played a lot of football in the playgrounds. Later, when my Dad became a committee member of the Watsonian Football Club, he used to run the line with the seconds, thirds and fourths on a Saturday afternoon. All his pals had kids roughly the same age and we used to go down to play football at Myreside. Nowadays, I see the children of my contemporaries, Euan Kennedy and Roger Baird, all doing the same things that we once did. Often it was freezing outside and pitch dark, yet there we were, playing with a rugby ball or a football, while our Dads were drinking up in the club house. Then it was a case of going off to the chippy and getting a fish supper on the way home, where we arrived absolutely filthy but happy.

As we got older, we used to play on the adjacent pitch at Myreside during Watsonians home matches but as soon as the goal kicks were being taken on the main pitch I would stop playing and go and watch the goal kickers, who fascinated me. We used to play a game called gaining ground, with two or more players in each team. It was simply a question of kicking the ball up field and making as much yardage as possible; if you caught the ball in field you were allowed to advance ten yards and punt it, and, as soon as you were within goal kicking range, you could place the ball and attempt to kick it between the posts for a score. I probably had more success then than I had in 1994 in the Five Nations Championship!

We started playing rugby in primary six, when we were ten years old, but for me it all began disastrously, for one day I was playing football in the school playground when a teacher drove past where he should not have been. I collided with his car, ripped my leg and needed about 15 stitches inserted in the wound. I was devastated, for I missed my first couple of months of rugby. But there is always a silver lining – the teacher whose car I collided with was the rugby master in charge of our year. Within about a week of starting he had made me captain of the side, which was very amusing and showed that he had a conscience. Luck, it seemed, was always on my side, and that year we played seven games and won all seven matches.

During the next few years we played all the other rugby-playing schools in Scotland, as well as our Edinburgh rivals, Stewart's Melville and Heriot's, and we always seemed to have close matches. Strangely, not many of us progressed from that era and only David Sole and myself advanced from our contemporaries all the way through from the Scottish schoolboys team to the full national side. It is amazing when you see players who had so much talent at school suddenly lose their ambition when they leave and discover beer, women and work. I guess they have found different priorities in their lives, but I thought that many of them wasted their natural resources. I can never understand why people do not make the most of their innate talent and work hard to fully develop their potential. After all, life is not a dress rehearsal, it is for real.

I began to understand and commit myself to rugby pretty seriously when I got into the first XV in my fifth year, which was probably the norm; the better fifth year players always made it into the first XV. Getting into the firsts when I was sixteen was a great thrill. I was playing stand off in those days, for all my early rugby was played in that position, but then I got injured in a midweek game and went to Donald Scott (Mr Scott or Sir, in those days) who was in charge of the school first XV, and told him that I did not think I could play at stand off. We were short with a couple of injuries, so he said, 'I'll play you at full back', and I have been there ever since. I have a lot to thank Donald Scott for, that is for sure.

Donald Scott had ten caps for Scotland in the early Fifties, and played in the infamous 44–0 disaster against the Springboks in 1951. I am afraid that was superseded by our recent 51–15 beating by the All Blacks. We never reminded Donald about the Springboks match when we were at school, for he was a ruthless teacher. I remember that once he got out a belt, two inches wide and about half an inch thick, and said, 'If there is any messing around, this is what is going to happen', then proceeded to take a chunk out of a very thick mahogany door. Bloody hell! There was no messing about after that. Donald was a strict teacher, but he was a good man. He used to run one of the school boarding houses and all the boys from Donald's bug hut, as we used to call his house, were fairly well behaved.

It was Graeme, my older brother, who set the standard for us to follow when he got capped in 1978 for the Scottish schools side, but it is difficult to decide when I harboured the ambition to go all the way in rugby. I suppose it began with John Rutherford, who was a PE teacher at Watson's at that time, and after I was made captain of the first XV, which was the first of many great honours given to me.

John Rutherford was playing for Scotland at the time, and I remember going down to the main pitch at Myreside with this fantastic rugby player who was to become a legend; but in those days he could not kick a rugby ball all that well, so I was able to help him. I felt that I had something to do with improving his kicking and, therefore, assisting his famous career! In fact we benefited from each other because he was a fantastic tactician. He would phone me up or come and see me and say, 'Come on, we'll go and practise kicking', and he would put up some high balls under the posts, as he would in a game, and I would try and catch them and return them to touch. We also used to play the gaining ground game, and the fact that, at the end of his career, he was a marvellous kicker of the rugby ball was purely down to the dedication and the hard work he put in. He was one of the greatest Scottish players of all time, a super guy and it was a real pleasure to have known and played with him.

Unfortunately, his career was cut short when he got injured in a game, the Easter classic in Bermuda, an annual jamboree organised by a bunch of Irish and Scottish guys. John went out there a couple of months before the World Cup and, calamitously, he wrecked his knee and really was not fit for the World Cup, which was a tragedy for Scotland.

Of course John was only a young lad then and not much older than us schoolboys when he was first capped in 1979. You could see on his face the delight of being picked for Scotland, and this told me that this was the next stage for me, so to speak. It took me six years of hard work to get there.

To many of my friends, who have pulled my leg over the years, I would like to say that at school I was scholastically better than average. I got six Highers. In Scotland, Highers are just slightly below 'A' Levels. I personally think that it is harder to study six subjects over two years than the three you may be required to do in 'A' Levels. I got reasonably good grades, three B's and three C's, and that was fine. When I went to see the Careers Tutor at the end of my fifth year, he asked me what I wanted to do and I told him that I was interested in property and architecture or surveying. He said, 'You are going to need a couple more Highers for that', so I sat two more in my last year at Watson's, which does not sound much, but others in their last year did a hell of a lot less.

The sixth year at school was great fun, for the girls were there, so we discovered them and went out with them, and everything else, which made it a very exciting time. Apart from rugby I was also playing cricket, and played in the school's first XI for three years. I also played squash and golf for the school teams. I was always doing something different and it was a lovely light-hearted time of my life, with little or nothing to worry about.

From school I went to Paisley College of Technology to read Land Economics and I can remember my first day of further education, and my Dad dropping me off at the station very early in the morning. I think I was still asleep, for I jumped on a train which eventually arrived in a station called Carstairs, where there is a large mental hospital, which is where I ought to have been, because after a further hour I realised that I should have arrived in Glasgow long since. Finally the ticket collector came along, looked at my ticket and said, 'Where are you off to, son?' Sheepishly I told him Paisley, and he said, 'No you're not, you're on the Birmingham train.' Eventually I got off at Carlisle for a train back to Glasgow and then another to Paisley. I arrived just as morning classes were finished, so I spent my first day at College either on the train or in the pub with my classmates, and some would say that matters did not improve much after that beginning.

Paisley was the sort of college that people attended during the week, went to classes and then disappeared at the weekends, so socially it was not the best place I could have gone to. Nevertheless I enjoyed it, for it was an interesting and different experience. We used to go away on field trips to places like St Andrews and London, and once even to Dublin. It was similar to going on a rugby tour and, with young guys and girls away together, it was great fun, and we were up at all hours messing around.

I came back at the weekends to play for Watsonians and was soon involved in the Edinburgh and Scottish Under-21 sides. There was always a tremendous amount of rugby going on and I played far more rugby in those early days than I would ever dream of now.

I got my BSc after four years' hard toil, including one year out working for Kenneth Ryden and Partners, Chartered Surveyors in Edinburgh, and I thought it was a bit too early to start in the real world. So, having been fascinated watching the Varsity match on television, I fancied going to Cambridge University for a couple of years to enjoy the things that I felt I had missed out on, from a social point of view, at Paisley. I went to the Head of Department, who was ex-Cambridge and who knew a Professor Millington at the University, and he encouraged me to apply as he thought it would be good for me. How right he was!

During the Seventies and early Eighties, the University match had been going to the dogs, to the extent that one year they had a mere 17,000 spectators. Consequently certain members of the University decided to do something about it, and, in order to beef up the Cambridge rugby side, they adopted a policy of taking in postgraduates. Fortunately for me, the principal vehicle they used for this purpose was Land Economy. A stream of us have followed that route, players such as Huw Davies, Rob Andrew, Richard Moon, Mark Thomas, Mike Hall, Marcus Rose, Chris Oti, Andrew Harriman, John Ellison and many more. I therefore spoke to people such as Ian Robertson, who was assisting with coaching Cambridge at the time, and was advised to apply for Magdalene College. After a strenuous interview I was accepted.

Again I was lucky, because one of the principal moving lights in putting Cambridge rugby back on the map was Dr Colin Kolbert, who was a Fellow of Magdalene. He resigned his Fellowship when Magdalene introduced female students into the College, because he felt that in such a small college it would dilute the strength of the sport, and the rugby in particular, to an absurd degree. Colin Kolbert was a very strong and proud man who would always uphold his own thoughts and principles. He was one of life's real gentlemen and a tremendous supporter of both College and University rugby and University life in general. He put things in perspective for us all and certainly left us in no doubt that, while it was important to play rugby for the University, it was just as important and extremely essential that we kept up with our studies. He was a pleasant man, very popular and easy to get on with, as well as being highly intelligent. We all respected him and enjoyed having a beer with him after the games.

One of the other stable influences, upholding and achieving the continuity and traditions of Cambridge rugby, is another administrator, Chris Taylor, who had a drive within him that wanted to make things work. Tony Rodgers is another great man who manages and coaches the technical side of things. Other committee men of the time, such as Dr Tony Craigen and John Dingle are terrific guys, and it is all these dedicated men who make Cambridge rugby tick; without them the University would be a far poorer place.

Cambridge was probably the best thing that ever happened

to me. When I first arrived, I felt an outsider and very naive. I realised that I spoke differently from most people who were there but, once I got settled into the rugby scene, I soon found my feet. I arrived a couple of weeks early and was given a lovely room in College, a graduate room. I was very comfortable there. We trained every day and I quickly got to know everybody and began to have a fantastic time.

Tony Rodgers was the backbone of the rugby coaching, but we occasionally had guest coaches. One was Ian Robertson, who played eight times for Scotland at stand off between 1968 and 1970. He came up two or three times during the Michaelmas term and I always remember that he had the oldest boots you had ever seen, a really old Adidas track suit and an antique rugby jersey, but his hair was always immaculate. He would say, 'Right, boys, up and down the field 20 times and pass the ball', so we did this religiously and then he would start slagging us off one by one. This was Ian's method of coaching us and it obviously worked because we won the Varsity match by 32–6. The thing about Ian was that he was quite a comedian and great fun, and his infectious humour always seemed to settle us. Ian had some great players to coach, for the back division that year was Richard Moon, Rob Andrew, Kevin Simms, Fran Clough, Mark Bailey and Andy Martin; and in the forwards we had John Ellison, Ian Morrison and Sean O'Leary, who all became top-class forwards.

With such a back division, in 1984 we won very easily and the back play was so good that we took a considerable step towards re-igniting interest in University rugby, but the crowd was still only some 30,000 compared with the 63,000 present in 1994. I felt that year was the beginning of the new hype for the Varsity match, which makes it a lovely day out and which empties the City of London – for that those marvellous sponsors, Bowring, must also take a bow.

I will always remember my first Varsity match. We stayed at the Petersham Hotel, Richmond, where the England team also stay, and we had a bus driver, Alan Nixon, who was a delightful man. We had tremendous journeys, and Alan would not care what time we got back to Cambridge as long as we had a bloody good booze-up on the way home. He was a great guy, a football man through and through, but he seemed to get great joy from looking after us and became totally converted to rugby, to the extent that we gave him the Cambridge sweater and a plaque for his bus.

I remember going to Twickenham along the A316 with a

police escort. The cars were nose to tail, so Alan just took his bus out and went down the other side of the dual carriageway at about 60 miles an hour. The theme tune from *Rocky*, *Eye of the Tiger*, was blaring out of the speakers, and I can recall being very psyched up on that journey. It really was one of the great experiences of a lifetime. After the game, we went off to the Oxford and Cambridge Club in Pall Mall for a cocktail party and then to dinner. One of the unusual things about the Varsity match is that Cambridge and Oxford always hold a separate dinner. We then met up at a ball organised by the Vincent's Club, but we were so drunk by the time we got there that I do not even know where it was. A great day and a memorable moment in my life!

We were, of course, fitter than we had ever been in our lives; only on a Lions Tour do you achieve that standard again. We trained every day in the afternoon, doing our work in the mornings and in the evenings, but I have to say that, if you are in the running for a Blue, then work tends to take second place – it is certainly not the main priority during the Michaelmas term. There is nothing wrong with that, in my opinion, as long as you realise that you have got to catch up in the next two terms. That is all part of disciplining yourself, which I think rugby players are good at.

The Varsity match is at the end of the Michaelmas term, and the Spring term is always a bit of an anti-climax. After all, we had been living in each others' kit bags for eight weeks and we had all become extremely close. After breaking up for Christmas for four or five weeks, we returned and then it was all a bit of a rush to select the captain for the next year. Usually there is some lobbying or at least sussing out who is interested in going for the captaincy. I was quite keen, for I had captained my school side and the Scottish school side, so I knew I had something to offer.

I suppose in a way we each put forward a manifesto, but I do not think I made any promises of free haggis or copious amounts of Scotch whisky if ever we were on tour! Anyway, I was made captain and in the Easter term we played sides like the Services and invitation teams like the Anti Assassins and the Luddites, but they are fairly irrelevant compared with the importance of the games leading up to the Varsity match in the autumn.

In my second year, I had a pretty good side and everybody said all we had to do was turn up at Twickenham to win. We were red-hot favourites with another good back division, for now we had Andy Harriman joining Fran Clough, Kevin Simms and Mark Bailey in the three-quarter line and a solid pack. We played some

In pensive mood prior to a Watsonians home match

With my first ball – before I could walk!

Me aged 13 (front row, third from right) at George Watson's College with Mr Cowan the coach and some serious-looking individuals

Mum and her boys. From left to right: Scott, Ewan, Gavin and Graeme, summer 1968

25 years on at Dad's 60th birthday party. From left to right: Dad and Mum flanking Corey with Gavin and Diane, Ewan, Jenny and Scott, Jacqui and Graeme

The team that won Scotland's first-ever victory on English soil at schoolboy level

Captain of Cambridge, 1985

Scoring for Cambridge in the 1984 Varsity match

I win my first cap with Scott, January 1986 v. France at Murrayfield (photograph: Bob Thomas)

On the charge in Cardiff with Scott in close support, 1986 (photograph: Colorsport)

Auckland University, 1987 – Gallacher Shield winners

Rugby life in New Zealand: Scotland v. All Blacks, 1990 (photograph: Colorsport)

Singapore Sevens heaven: (top) getting in some alternative training with Richard Cramb and Mark Thomas; (bottom) on tour with my employers of the time, Richard Ellis. Michael Lynagh is front right next to Richard Cramb of Scotland

pretty good games leading up to the Varsity match, including a victory over Mickey Steele-Bodger's XV by scoring two tries in the last three minutes and kicking the conversions. Unfortunately, there was an injury to Mark Thomas, who was playing stand off. He was a great pal of mine who had come up from Swansea and spoke in a funny Welsh accent, but gradually Cambridge knocked off the rough edges. He would have been the biggest outside half in the history of the Varsity match at about six foot four, and 14½ stone. He was a full back, but due to the lack of a fly half he was pressed into service because he had good hands and an enormous left-footed kick. He sustained a stupid injury, tearing his knee ligament with nobody near him. He was carried off and missed the Varsity match, but happily for him played in the next two years, once at full back and then on the wing, when, to everybody's delight, he scored the winning try.

Anyway, Mark Bailey moved from the left wing to stand off for the last quarter and did very well, but we were a bit fooled by his one-off performance and picked him at outside half for the Varsity match. With the benefit of hindsight, we would not have made that mistake again. We lost the match, 7–6, in front of 40,000 people, and I was a deeply disappointed man. You have to understand that your sole purpose during that term is to play well and win the Varsity match. It was everything – at the time it was our total *raison d'être* and we were all prepared to die for the cause. We were very fit and to lose that game as favourites was a crushing experience. I remember that Alan Jones, the Australian coach, who took the Wallabies to their first ever Grand Slam against the four Home Unions, had been brought in to coach the Oxford side. He worked wonders with them, mentally as well as physically, and he got the Oxford players to believe in themselves so much that they really pressured us. They played far better than we thought they were capable of and things did not run for us, but that is typical of Varsity rugby.

Nothing went right for us in that game and perhaps the precedent had been set some eight days earlier, when Bowring, the sponsors, held their traditional Press conference prior to the match in their plush city offices, when the two teams for the Varsity match were announced. As captain, it was my job to announce the Cambridge team and with my players behind me, facing the *Rugby Special* cameras and all the rugby journalists, I began; number 15, Gavin Hastings, number 14, Andy Harriman, number 13, Fran Clough, and went through the team, until I came to number six, and for some reason, although the bloke was standing right beside me, I could not get his name out. I knew him really well, having played with him all term, and yet the name simply would not come out. It seemed like an eternity as I struggled in front of the bright lights and the team began giggling behind me. Eventually, someone, I think it was Fran Clough, came to my aid and whispered his name in my ear, Steve Kelly, and, relieved, I announced his name before finishing the rest of the team. It was a most uncomfortable few moments and an occasion which the Cambridge guys never let me forget, but, again, I learnt from the experience and I have got more used to, and more confident in, handling the Press since that occasion.

I remember Steve Pearson playing brilliantly at scrum half for Oxford as they tore into a 7–0 lead, and it became hugely exciting for the crowd as we clawed our way back to 7–6. But they held out against terrific pressure. The tackling of their back row and their centres, Risman and Rydon, was decisive and ended a lean period for Oxford, who previously had suffered five successive defeats.

I had a whole lot of people, mostly mates of mine from Watsonians, on a mini-tour to watch the game. They thought the Varsity match was a great occasion; they were disappointed for me, but only for about five minutes afterwards, and it did not stop them having a hell of a good time. Once I had got over the initial disappointment, I, too, had a good night, and surely that is how it should be even in major competitive sport. Win or lose, the best of it is the taking part followed by the post-mortem and the reminiscences afterwards.

Traditionally, the captain has to make a speech. I thought I did not really want to do that, and felt it should be a more light-hearted occasion; so, a couple of weeks beforehand, I went into a joke shop in Cambridge and picked out different sorts of jokes that would apply to every single person in the team. That night, at our team dinner, I remember being well filled up with booze and I had this massive bag, which I dipped into. There was a big pair of Prince Charles ears and I told a wee story before giving them to Steve Kelly, a guy with big sticking-out ears. Our coach, Tony Rodgers, was a very amusing guy with terrible hair, one of the scruffiest and ugliest men in the world and I know he would not mind my saying that. One day before the Steele-Bodger's game his hair, for once, was absolutely immaculate, slicked down and beautifully combed to one side, but when he turned around you could see he had a big lump of mousse, which he had obviously borrowed from his wife, stuck behind his ear. Ever since then we called him Moose Head, so from my bag I dug out a baseball cap with a huge pair of antlers. Blindfolding Tony, we sat him at the top table and placed the hat on his head and the whole place collapsed with laughter. Kevin Simms, who had been giving us a spot of trouble all year, was handed a couple of plastic jobbies, so jokingly I said, 'These are for you because you've been a bit of a shit all season.'

It was all harmless fun and it was my way of speaking to the guys, saying well done, and endorsing all the glorious times we had enjoyed together. They are still amongst my best pals. Cambridge was important to me because it helped carry me forward into the next stage of my life. I think I was lucky to go there as a graduate and, being slightly older, I think I got far more out of Cambridge than most people. I was not there to get a First or a Two One; I was there first and foremost to be a beneficiary of the variety of experiences that Cambridge had to offer and, if that included rugby, then that was fine. It did include rugby, but I still got my degree and I have no qualms about telling people why I was at Cambridge, and that I got a hell of a lot out of it and thoroughly enjoyed the experience.

The Varsity match is valuable because it raises the profile of both Oxford and Cambridge Universities. We felt that as rugby players we were helping to promote the University. Cambridge enabled and taught me to get on with people from many different walks of life and, because I was brought up differently from a lot of those who went to Cambridge, it proved to be a stimulating and inspiring learning experience for me.

Grange Road, the University rugby ground, is a beautiful place to play rugby as it has wonderful environment all around it and, in the delightful ambience of having tea in the pavilion, you can relate to the great players who have appeared there. On the walls inside the pavilion are all the Varsity teams that have played over the years. When you see your own name in gold leaf lettering up there among so many demi-gods, such as Wavell Wakefield, Carl Aarvold, the Bedell-Sivright brothers, Wilf Wooller, Ken Fyfe, Mike Gibson, Arthur Smith, Ken Scotland and many others, then it is a very proud feeling. It is élitist, but that is one of the charms of such a place, and if you are lucky enough to go there then that is your good fortune; it is not the only élitist place in the world.

You must take Cambridge for what it is and not what you think it will be. I went down there with a very open mind and did not know what to expect, but without question came away having had the best two years of my life. There were so many good people and so many different interests and opportunities. For instance, I had never rowed before, so I joined the graduate boat at Magdalene for the May Bumps. The Cambridge bumping races are an incredible experience and a fabulous festival of fun. They are also extremely hard work; I mean it was the hardest sport I had ever done. I was used to picking up a squash racquet or a golf club and being reasonably competent, but here I had to learn and employ completely new skills and techniques. I got caught up in the different lifestyle of being a boatie. We used to go drinking with all the guys who rowed for Cambridge that year, and John Pritchard, a great pal of mine, was the stroke of the Blue boat and rowed in the 1984 Los Angeles Olympics. What a lovely guy! We knew how hard they trained and we were all behind them, and they in turn reciprocated and supported the rugby team.

I also played a couple of games for the University Golf Team and I like to think that I could have won a golf Blue, but often the two sports coincided and I could not commit myself to golf; but, like the rowers, the golf boys were also a great bunch to know and were not averse to having a drink or two.

Yes, I think what captured my imagination most at that time were the delightful and highly amusing people I met at Cambridge. You really could not meet better blokes than Richard Moon, Rob Heginbotham, Mark Bailey, Fran Clough, Kevin Simms, Kelvin Wyles, Trevor Borthwick and Andy Harriman, and all the others I played with. Andy, the Nigerian, was a special player and terrific fun to go on tour with. As long as people like Andy go through Oxford and Cambridge, the Varsity matches will live for ever. I am always keen to encourage up-and-coming rugby talent to go there and have the joy of the Cambridge experience. Of course, much depends on the admission tutors letting them in, because the scholastic levels are so high these days. The demands of attending lectures or whatever are not huge and, therefore, there is a big onus on the individual to study on his own. Many people go off the rails, but I reckon all the rugby players I knew had the discipline to succeed where other people fell by the wayside.

Work apart, we had tremendous fun. At the May Bumps, after which we had the Bump supper, there was a riotous party. Magdalene College boathouse was to be demolished on the Monday, so we left the college bar at midnight and decided to go down to the Fen and give the demolition an early start. We were wearing our dinner jackets and black ties, and we started chucking a few stones at the windows. All of a sudden people started jumping out of the woods. It was the hit squad of the local police! We were arrested and put in the cells at one o'clock in the morning, and only let out at half past five. It was just harmless, stupid fun and high spirits, and although we were not charged by the police, we had to explain ourselves to the tutors and we each had to pay a small fine.

Coming back in the bus from away games, we used to have Captain's Cocktails. We would stop at an off-licence and buy half-bottles of various spirits and go around mixing them in plastic cups. We invented some really nauseous drinks and I often wondered how we managed to consume so much alcohol and still get up early for training the next day without feeling too ill. I suppose it was one of the joys of being young.

Two days before the Varsity match, it was tradition that we ate at Doc Dingle's house, where he and his wife have hosted lunch for the last 20 years. The players have always failed to eat her out of food, even though we were offered, and had, doubles and trebles of everything. We had roast beef, pork, lamb and then on to the desserts, probably about 20 of them, trifle, apple crumble, lemon meringue pie, bread and butter pudding and so on. I am sure people would say it was the biggest meal they ever ate in their lives and basically the guys did not eat between that Sunday lunchtime and the Varsity match, because they were absolutely stuffed. We drank a few wines, but did not go overboard; it was all very civilised and it helped wind us down prior to the big game.

The next day, on the Monday morning, we had our final training session and we travelled down to Richmond in the afternoon, totally focused on the game. Again, these are memories that will live forever.

There was, of course, the lighter side of Cambridge and almost every college had its drinking club. At Magdalene it was called the Wyvern Club, and they were always very keen to have us sportsmen on board. The Wyverns were like a lot of drinking clubs in the different colleges, with initiation ceremonies to get through. Ours was an innocuous affair; I think we had to drink a pint and a half of bitter, a pint of snakebite (half lager and half cider), and a pint of lager with a tomato juice in it. We used to put a bucket in front of those who were being initiated. Fortunately, I was one of the guys who could keep their drink inside their body, but when you have got someone else depositing their excesses in the bucket and it is wafting in front of your nose when you are trying to down your own pint, it is fairly off-putting. I managed to get mine down in about 35 seconds, a record, which was subsequently beaten at the next initiation by one of the boaties, Paddy Broughton.

The Wyverns had a cocktail party every term and we would invite members of other drinking clubs from the different colleges, and they would reciprocate. One night I got absolutely shafted because, whenever anybody came up to you, clinked your glass and said 'Amigo' or 'Bumper', you had to down it in one. Luckily we did not drink out of huge glasses, only wine glasses, but if you had to do 30 bumpers, as I did that evening, then you finished up not feeling too well.

On another occasion, I was at the St John's College drinking club and there were some eggs flying around. There were a couple of boaties there wearing their blazers. I always used to think it was very pretentious for someone to wear the blue blazer awarded when you won a full Blue against Oxford University. John Pritchard was there and an egg went flying through the air, landed on his jacket and cracked open. He immediately came over and threatened to kick the shit out of me. I wondered what the hell he was doing and proclaimed my innocence. The sequel to this was that I got a letter from him in the summer of 1993 when I was in New Zealand, with condolences after our first Test defeat. He added that, after eight years of being convinced it was I who threw that egg (for which he had sent me a cleaning bill, which I paid although I was innocent), he had since discovered the real culprit and he was sorry for giving me such a hard time and falsely accusing me for all those years.

There was one day called Suicide Sunday when there were six or seven of these drinking parties, and people used to see how far they could go. The first one started about ten in the morning and the last one would be eight o'clock in the evening. If you survived the day, you were doing very well indeed because of the excesses of all the bumpering.

You always had to wear your Wyvern tie every Monday and that tradition is for life. If you come up against any member, say in the centre of London, and are not wearing your tie and get caught out, you have to buy them a pint. I get caught all the time because I do not even know where my Wyvern tie is. The marvellous thing about Cambridge was that the experience would last for a lifetime and our predecessors, men such as Huw Davies and Marcus Rose, who left Cambridge just before me, set standards for us all to follow. I cannot speak too highly of men like Fran Clough, Richard Moon, Mark Bailey, Kevin Simms, Andy Harriman and the rest of the Cambridge team. Cloughie was a real character, a Lancashire man from near Wigan, who was a very fine player, a hard man with immense determination. Strangely, he was not actually thought of as highly as he should have been and he should have won more caps for England. Cloughie and I were always competitive with each other. On and off the field we were often in confrontation, not in the physical way, but he was one of those guys who liked to wind people up and if he could get one over on you he was satisfied. But, like many of his ilk, he hated being wound up himself.

Richard Moon was another close pal, this tiny little guy invariably sun-tanned because always, it seemed, he had come back from a couple of weeks in some exotic place. He may have been a wee guy but he was a bundle of courage and skill. We lived near each other and we became the firmest of friends and shared many laughs. Then there was Kelvin Wyles, another great friend, a bit of an oddball and always a bit lighter headed than the rest of us, but a real competitor. Mark Bailey was an extraordinarily amusing character and a good man. He was playing for England and was captain of Cambridge before me. Although he was injured for most of that Michaelmas term, he got himself fit for the Varsity match in 1984 and played extremely well. Mark was very intelligent and, as a graduate, was doing his PhD at the time. The story goes that he went up to my parents and made some comment, like, 'You've got another son who's a good rugby player. Is he coming to Cambridge?' My old man, in his sort of serious manner, said, 'No, no, Gavin's the intellectual of our family.' Bloody hell! Talk about a line that was going to haunt me for the rest of my Cambridge days, then that was it. Clough, Bailey, Rodgers and Co made great capital of that and when they needed to give Hastings a bit of stick at cocktail parties, which they certainly did, people like Tony Rodgers would cast aspersions on my intelligence.

Andy Harriman who, as captain, almost single-handedly propelled England to winning the World Cup Sevens in Edinburgh, is another great friend. He was doing the same course, so we saw a great deal of each other. He is a Nigerian prince and has oodles and oodles of money, but he was never pretentious and was always charming and polite to anybody, no matter who they were.

He used to drive his Porsche around Cambridge when most of us were on bikes. Once I got a lift back from rugby training and he said, 'Look into my glove compartment and pick out a tape.' When I opened it, a pile of parking tickets flew out at me. He used to put his car bang outside the lecture rooms and pick up about four parking tickets every day. I do not know if he ever paid them but he did not seem to be too bothered. He had a phone installed in his rooms and would make lots of calls to Nigeria and all over the world. I remember when he was away on a trip somewhere and someone sharing his digs complained about the amount of money he had spent on the phone. The bill came to something like four hundred pounds, and this guy kicked up absolute hell about it. Calmly, Andy went into his wallet and said quite casually, 'Will cash do?' He was a lovely man, also a real ladies man, a great personality in every sense of the word, but a fine gentleman. He was a bit quick too, and a truly tremendous Sevens player. Andy really made his mark in the 1993 World Cup Sevens, and the way he went around David Campese, with bags of pace and confidence, was one of the great memories of the tournament. He only had one cap, against Australia in 1988 when, again, Campese got no change from him. I thought he was hard done by and should have been capped more times for England.

We have got a huge Cambridge Mafia going and, in the years ahead, we are going to go on bumping into each other and remembering the good times, which is what life is all about. Your real friends are people whom you do not have to speak to on a regular basis. You can meet them ten years later and take on from where you left off. Cambridge was all part of the experience of life and I would not have missed it for the world. You have got to make the most of these opportunities because you never know what is going to happen, and no one can ever accuse me of not making the most of my chances through rugby. I have done an awful lot and seen much of the world, and I have had many good times along with the bad. It was the occasional hard times that taught me to grow up and to enjoy the good times even more.

CHAPTER III

Brothers in Arms

THE HASTINGS CLAN are a close and happy family, well known for their loyalty and devotion to each other. My mother, Isobel, could perhaps be described as an archetypal matriarch, for she has had an immense influence on our lives, while my father, Clifford, himself no mean rugby player for Watsonians, is more laid back. Although generally more critical of his brood, he has spent his life running after us and securing our future. Mum is probably our most avid fan; her kitchen is a gallery of press cuttings, which she proudly shows to all her visitors.

We are four brothers; Graeme, the eldest by two years, myself, Scott, three years my junior, and Ewan, two years behind him. Scott and I were in the middle and, therefore, were left to fend for ourselves most of the time. My mother tells me that there was an antagonistic rivalry between Graeme and me, and my relationship with Scott was not particularly friendly, either, in the early days. However, as we grew up we all came closer together and now we are pretty supportive of each other, without animosity or envy.

We used to follow the soccer results every Saturday after the rugby. Graeme and Scott supported Hibs, while I supported Hearts and, therefore, when there was an Edinburgh derby match and Hearts won, which they usually did, I was not particularly popular with them. I enjoyed rubbing it in.

It was often quite funny when Scott and I were on tour as brothers, when we got the inevitable fines for forming a clique.

41

Over the years we had to be careful about saying too much to each other, or sharing a quiet moment, a quiet beer, or having any in-depth conversations on tour, because, if we were found out, we were always fined and it used to cost us a fortune. Therefore, as brothers, we have never roomed with each other, which was a blessing in disguise, and also, because the Scottish management had a structure that a back always shared with a forward, we never needed to justify it either.

Nevertheless, being such a close-knit family, we would seize a chance to break away from the touring party and I can recall during the World Cup in 1987, when Graeme had come across from Australia and our parents had come out to support Scotland, that we had a great party in a bar in the Central Square in Christ-church. So there we were, Mum, Dad, Graeme, Scott and myself, five out of six of the Hastings clan, standing on the other side of the world, having a few beers. What a delight it was! The great thing was that we also had an entourage of Scottish supporters and a number of our New Zealand friends, whom Scott and I had met on previous trips abroad. This was a classic example of one of the great pleasures of rugby, relaxing and having a drink with family and friends, and being there because of the World Cup.

I think we were very lucky, with our parents being very supportive and the fact that we grew up as young kids in a big, family house not very far from the school, George Watson's College, where we were all educated. It was a tremendous com-mitment by my father to send us all to a private school, which was noted for its sporting, as well as its scholastic, excellence, and we were encouraged by our parents to become fully involved in everything. They were always ferrying us around with our school chums, either to golf courses or to rugby matches, and when we used to go for family walks to places like the Braid Hills, we would always take a rugby ball or a football. Even then we were very competitive with each other and Dad was always prompting us by saying, 'Remember your left foot' and 'don't forget your weaker foot', and 'you must pass both ways'. It did not matter whether it was rugby, football, cricket, rounders, golf or anything else, he was always egging us on to improve our performance. If it was winter, it was rugby and soccer; when Wimbledon came, it would be out with our tennis racquets, and during the British Open it would be out with the golf clubs. Whatever sporting event was on at the time, we would all be taking an interest in it.

It was during our schoolboy days that we began to make our

first rugby contacts and to build our future network, meeting the likes of David Sole, playing for Glenalmond. Stuart Barnes played against us both for Welsh Schools and Phillipe Sella for French Schools, and Scott played against Steve Tuynman, who played and captained Australian Schools at Murrayfield in 1984, and literally five months later won his full Australian cap. I followed my elder brother, Graeme, into the Scottish Schoolboys side, and Scott followed me, so that was our first real taste of representative football. As usual, Mum and Dad supported all our games. They even took the trouble to go over to Cork in the Republic of Ireland to see Scott captain the Scottish Schoolboys against the Irish Schoolboys, who were captained by Brendan Mullin, now a good friend of ours. Those were salad days for the young Hastings family.

We were very lucky to be part of such a happy, albeit competitive, household, where our parents took a prolonged, consistent and active interest in our wellbeing. As youngsters we always had *au pair* girls to look after us and, looking back at family photographs at some pretty attractive, blonde bombshells, it seems a shame that we were too young to appreciate who was bathing us.

It is quite extraordinary that, although Scott and I won our first caps together in 1986 and also achieved the amazing statistic of winning our 50th caps together against France at the end of the 1994 season, we had not played much rugby together prior to that, and to this day have never played against each other. It was only in college holidays that we occasionally had the opportunity to play alongside each other. However, since 1986 we have been on so many rugby tours and enjoyed so many good times together that we have now developed a tremendous bond of friendship and I cannot tell you how much I have enjoyed playing alongside Scott. To me, he has always been a bit of a character, a bit of a nutcase if you like, because he has always been a little more on the wild side than myself. Thankfully, since he got married and Corey, his son, arrived, he has mellowed a wee bit, which is a relief and something that at one time I never thought possible. He was the crazy horse of the family, as befits a guy who once let off a firework rocket in the kitchen! Well, I think he was, but my older brother Graeme would give him a close run for his money.

Scott is rock solid in defence and there is probably no-one better in world rugby at chasing the high ball. There are few better defenders than him, for he is very strong and committed in the tackle, sometimes over-committed, like the time he damaged his jaw and cheekbone on the 1993 Lions tour, an injury that caused him to fly home early on in the tour, which was very disappointing for us all.

Scott has always been an extremely sociable and flamboyant personality, and one of the real characters in world rugby, who is popular wherever he goes. He knows how to enjoy himself but, by the same token, he also knows when to button up his mouth and knuckle down to the job in hand. He even occasionally listens to me!

You sometimes have a vision of a person and when you actually meet them in the flesh they never quite come up to your expectations, but I do not think the same could be said of Scott, for he probably exceeds any expectations you may have of him as a player or as a person enjoying himself off the field. My other two brothers, Graeme and Ewan, have always had a lower profile, but Graeme, who has lived in Australia for many years, also played rugby to a good standard and has played for his state side, Victoria, against a number of New Zealand touring teams. He has also been on tour in New Zealand and played against Provincial sides, like Counties. He even played against Sean Lineen, when he was an up-and-coming young buck, in the Bombay Hills. Ewan, in turn, has played a number of games for Watsonians, although he is more regularly seen in one of the lower sides.

Mum and Dad, of course, have travelled all over the world to see us play and I can never thank them enough, for I fully appreciate the support they have always given us. Ewan has thoroughly enjoyed and shared in some of the reflected glory, and I think that it must have been much harder for him, coming up behind Scott and myself, than it was for Graeme, to be on the fringes. Therefore, Ewan has probably had the hardest time, most of all from Scott. Nevertheless, having matured and grown older, he is quite happy to relish our success and, again, we are grateful to him and I cannot speak too highly of his support for us.

The old saying goes that behind every good man there is a great woman and this is certainly true of my wife, Diane, who has been my best friend ever since I met and dated her. Graeme's wife, Jacqui, and Scott's wife, Jenny, fit into the same mould and, together with Scott's son, Corey, are part of a big, happy family. Our parents have been marvellous at cooking for us, but it does not take long before the conversation around the dinner table comes back to rugby, and that is the way our life has been for the last 15 years. We have had a lot of fun out of it, not only Scott and myself but everyone associated with our lives.

I met Diane, I think, one lucky night in a bar, probably prior to a rugby match. Edinburgh is a fairly sociable place when it comes to drinking in the pubs, and you only need to be around the city for three or four years to know the places to go for a drink, and where you are liable to bump into some good-looking girls. I was lucky enough to bump into Diane at the right time, even though we knew each other a long time before we started going out. Perhaps if we had started our relationship in our early twenties it might not have worked out, because, to a young man, rugby and the opportunity to go touring all over the world is a great life and one that I took full advantage of. It would have been difficult if I had really felt for the person that I was going out with at the time and perhaps I would have worried more about going away. At the time I started going out with Diane, I had already seen a great deal of the world; I instinctively knew that she was the girl for me and that I was ready to give more to our relationship. I think everyone shows greater wisdom as they grow older and times and circumstances change. If you have a loved one back home, then you are not likely to do the things you might have done in earlier days, and that has certainly been true in my case. I am very content with our relationship, which is a very strong one, and I know that Diane thoroughly enjoys coming to all the International matches and meeting everybody. I could not be happier than I am at this time of my life, and she is the reason.

I am not, however, changing her from a rugby widow into a golf widow! I had the answer to that when I made her join a local golf club just before we were married, because I thought on the old adage: 'If you can't beat them, join them.' I knew that Diane would have talent on the golf course and I try to give her as much encouragement as possible. If we do not meet on the course, although we do occasionally, then we can always meet at the 19th hole!

I am always amazed when I hear that some rugby players, who play at the very top level, have partners who cannot stand the sport. Young players often require a very special person to marry and here again I am fortunate in having Diane, who is fairly athletic and keeps fit with aerobics and swimming. We have been playing mixed touch rugby in the summer, which she thoroughly enjoys, and this not only gives her a very good insight into rugby skills but gives me a chance to see the boys again.

To come back to Scott, I do not suppose that we have ever been as close as we have become over the last few years and when we celebrated that quite unique occasion of winning 50 caps together, we both took enormous pleasure in the achievement of the other. It really was a marvellous milestone in our lives and the Scottish Rugby Union generously gave us each a nice tankard to mark the event. It was also acclaimed by the national Press, as they too recognised that it was a very special event which was unlikely ever to happen again. However, records are there to be broken and I suppose, one day, it is possible that two other brothers can achieve what we have done. I only hope that they will have had as much pleasure and fun – and a little success along the way – as Scott and I have enjoyed.

The party was spoilt by the fact that it was the first time that we had lost to France at Murrayfield in our experience of five home encounters. It would have been so much more memorable if we had won and Scott had scored the winning try and I had kicked the winning goal, but that is life and by now both Scott and I have learnt to treat those two imposters, triumph and disaster, just the same. So we did have a few extra glasses of champagne and a tremendous sing-song in the hotel afterwards, for sometimes from the depths of defeat and despair come good times and optimism for the future. It was certainly true of that evening.

In many ways, Scott is even more competitive than I am, and sometimes on the rugby field he can become too aggressive and go into situations where he really should not have gone, when his desire and his instinct got the better of him. As an example of that, I recall when he played on the left wing for Scotland against the All Blacks and he got drawn in to tackle Frank Bunce, while the young New Zealand protégé, Jeff Wilson, was put in for a try. Our excuse would be that they should not have picked him on the wing in the first place, but there is no doubt that he always wants to be in the thick of the defensive action. However, more often than not he gets it right.

His other attribute as a rugby player is that he is extremely fierce and, together with endeavour, dedication and pride, this embraces the whole persona of Scott. He is also a very skilful player, as you would expect from a man who has played 50 times for his country and been selected for two Lions tours, but he will never be graced with the same pace or guile of a Jeremy Guscott, who, in turn, does not possess many of Scott's great qualities. Most International teams would be happy to have him playing in the centre and certainly Scotland can be thankful for his durability and consistency, and the fact that he has played so many times for them.

I feel that you know where you stand with Scott. I have a certain expectancy of him and a comfort level when he is out there in defence in front of me. He will always, however, be better known for his defensive qualities, for he has saved a hell of a lot of tries for Scotland, and perhaps his attacking qualities do not fully match up to his astonishing defensive attributes.

It is the ambition of neither of us to win more caps than the other but, as Scott is three years younger, then he has a bigger advantage in that respect. I have a feeling that, perhaps, we may just decide to hang up our boots at the same time, which could be after the World Cup in 1995. You can only commit yourself for as long as you go on enjoying and having fun out of it. We both have a driving ambition to play in the 1995 World Cup in South Africa and thus play in three World Cups. It would be great to have one last opportunity to play against the best in the world and, again, I would like to be known as the best full back of the 1995 World Cup.

It was for that reason that Scott and I decided not to go to Argentina in the summer of 1994, purely to give ourselves a more than even chance of going to South Africa in 1995. We had been playing rugby non-stop since 1988 and our bodies needed a rest. It is important to refresh the mind and to keep sharp because much of rugby nowadays is a mental game as much as a physical one. Physically, people are stronger, faster and fitter than before, but what you must also cultivate is a sharpness of mind. As soon as people become mentally tired, no matter how physically fit they are, they will not perform to their best on the rugby field.

That Scotland tour to Argentina was disappointing because there was insufficient development by the young players. I believe that players should perform to the best of their ability on such rugby tours, and those who failed in Argentina have no right to expect to get into a Scotland team. You must not let your eyes deceive you, you go on what you see on tour and there is no other way. You cannot tell me that if a player comes back after a poor tour and then, perhaps, plays reasonably well in some early season club matches, you can ignore what happened in Argentina. When you commit yourself solely to rugby on a tour and then you do not perform, it usually shows that you are not good enough; end of story.

The problem facing Scotland in the World Cup will be one of experience, for the younger players in Scotland will not get sufficient of the necessary standard of games to prepare them anything like adequately enough for the World Cup, by comparison with the way the other countries are developing their experience.

England, having gone to South Africa in the summer of 1994 on a traumatically difficult tour, which brought them one great Test victory followed by a horrendous defeat, will have learnt greatly from the experience. New Zealand had incoming tours by France and South Africa. Australia played Italy, Ireland, Western Samoa and New Zealand; while amongst the most battle-hardened troops in the World Cup should surely be the Welsh. During the summer of 1994 they played two World Cup qualifying games, against Portugal and Spain, then went on to Canada, Fiji, Tonga and Samoa, for four ferociously hard Tests, and then came back to play Romania and Italy, then South Africa and, finally, the Five Nations. That is one hell of a lot of Internationals! You certainly will not accuse Wales of not preparing adequately for the World Cup.

For all that, I think that England have had the best preparation by going to South Africa, for they will know exactly the problems of altitude, the state of the grounds, the travel of the ball through the thin air of the high veldt and the liveliness of the bounce on the hard grounds. Above all, they will have played against South African players and will know how quick, physically strong and aggressive they are likely to be.

I predict that South Africa will win the World Cup. Australia, France and New Zealand will also be very strong, and I think that England are capable of being equally powerful but they must change the way that they have been playing since the early Nineties. In the build-up to the World Cup, they have been playing a very negative game and will certainly not win the World Cup by playing that sort of game on the hard grounds of the high veldt in South Africa. The team that shows the most imagination, pace, strength, flair, aggression, discipline and commitment will win the World Cup. I think it will require all those qualities and, on their own patch, South Africa will be very hard to beat.

As Jim Telfer remarked to the Scottish players at the start of the World Cup season – 'The World Cup will be played in South Africa next May and June, but the winning of it begins now.' Both Scott and I are looking forward to our third World Cup campaign, that is, if we are selected.

CHAPTER IV

Flower of Scotland

AT THE OFFICIAL DINNER after winning my first cap against France we had steak and stuffed tomatoes and, when I turned my back, some of the players had piled their tomatoes on to my plate. I thought no more about it until the following week, when the President of the Scottish Rugby Union came into the changing rooms before a squad session for the Welsh game to tell us that he was disappointed at a very serious incident the week before, when a tomato had landed on the dinner jacket of an executive of the Royal Bank of Scotland, the sponsor for Internationals at Murrayfield. The President implied that the silly ass knew who he was, when someone elbowed me in the ribs, I think it was Gary Callander, and said, 'You shouldn't have done that.' With a suspicious look at me, but none the wiser, the President left us with the imperishable words, 'You're going to play Wales next, so make sure you stuff them, rather than chuck stuffed tomatoes at our sponsor.' To this day I do not think it was I who threw that tomato but it did not seem to harm me in terms of being picked for Scotland.

After the incident with the Scottish 'B' team, when I missed the plane back to Edinburgh, and then this little episode, I realised that I may have been on pretty thin ice as far as the Scottish Rugby Union were concerned. Happily, they held nothing against me; on the contrary they have always been marvellously supportive to me and the rest of the guys, which is why we have been such a happy family of players and committee.

If Cambridge University was a delight, and the British Lions tours of Australia and New Zealand and the World Cup of 1991 were the high points of my career, it was my time with Scotland which was the real guts of my rugby, which helped me develop to the subsequent heights. The whole nitty gritty of my rugby life has been playing for Scotland. Without question, it is where my most intimate friends are and I have been extremely fortunate in playing with some wonderful people in the Scottish team.

I have been on tour with many illustrious players and funny people, with the British Lions, the Barbarians and other selected teams, and they are totally different and unique in their own way, but there is a special feeling and pleasure about playing for Scotland at home in the Five Nations Championship. If I say that most of my closest pals in rugby are the people that I have played with in the Scottish team, as opposed to any other teams, it is because these friendships are bonded over a long period of time, and are due to hard work through the innumerable training sessions we have been involved in over the years. We soldiered together on tours to New Zealand in 1990 and in the World Cup in 1987, as well as Australia in 1992.

When you go on tour with Scotland to these countries, the demand and the effort required is far greater than with the British Lions, because obviously the Lions are a much stronger and better side. Therefore, the challenge to perform with your national side against teams like New Zealand is enormous. We went through the thick and thin of the good and the bad times, which helped forge a terrific camaraderie.

It is evident that Scotland and Ireland have a much shallower depth of talent than the other countries of the Five Nations, and, therefore, we have always got to make the most of our resources, take great care in identifying our best players and make sure that we have consistency and continuity in selection. I believe in having an undying trust and respect for each other in the team and, of all the Scottish sides in which I have been involved, I can honestly say that there has never been a rift between any of the players or the reserves. We have always managed to create an unrivalled team atmosphere and to build an amazing team spirit. Many times that has carried Scotland through, and often, when we were on the verge of defeat, it brought us victory. It is also true that the Scottish game in my time has been graced by some marvellous coaches, of whom I will talk elsewhere.

Of course I have had great disappointments as player and

50

captain, and none more than in the recent 1994 season, when we simply did not perform at all well. There is no doubt that Scotland are now going through a rebuilding process. It was my job as captain to try and get the other half dozen experienced players to pass on some of their expertise to the younger members of the team. We failed, for whatever reason, though it was not due to any lack of desire on our part or from any lack of effort. I think that the new players simply did not believe or know what we were talking about, and for that I shoulder some of the responsibility.

I was never consulted by the Scottish selectors concerning their selections, nor did I wish to be. The Scottish Rugby Union would not want to set a precedent. However, coloured by the bad Press reports concerning the performances of the Scottish front five during the Lions Tour, and largely by the excellent performance of the Scotland 'A' side, against the All Blacks the week before, one must now say that the selections for the first International match of the 1993/94 season, against New Zealand, were poor. I told the new players that, no matter what happened the previous week, they must understand and believe that Test match rugby is a completely different kettle of fish. Few of the new players selected understood what I was saying and it was only after the game, when we were absolutely humiliated, that they came up to me and said, 'Jeez, you were right.' I knew I was right, but we had made the mistake collectively and I was prepared to accept that, provided they learned and used the experience to good effect so that we could turn it to our advantage in the future. What concerns and worries me is that I simply do not know whether the players really use such a bitter experience and disappointment to the best effect. I am not sure if they are capable of learning as quickly as I want them to.

I would want to say that, despite all the criticism they received after the Lions tour, Kenny Milne, Paul Burnell and Andy Reed fought their way back into the Scottish team and performed with distinction. I am not surprised at that, for we Scots are a proud nation. This is illustrated in the many symbols of our nationhood, particularly in the kilts and bagpipes, which many say are designed to whip us into a frenzy. This, of course, is nonsense; they are merely to keep our distinctive identity in a very large world. Look at the Scots all over the world and throughout history. They have been a very successful people, abounding in great soldiers, missionaries and industrialists. Wherever you go in the world, you bump into the chairmen or chief executives of huge international companies and you find that they never forget their roots. Take for instance Willy Purves, who, as Head of the Hong Kong and Shanghai Bank, has recently taken over the Midland Bank. He is one of the most powerful men in Hong Kong, yet every year when Scottish players arrive for the Hong Kong Sevens, he entertains them lavishly because he is so proud to be Scottish.

We played the first match of the 1987 World Cup against France in Christchurch, and all we could hear in the changing-rooms was the skirl of bagpipes playing out on the paddock. When you are on the other side of the world and you hear such potent Scottish symbolism, then it gives you a tremendous lift. It is probably difficult for less clannish people to realise the depth of feeling and the raising of the spirits which it inspires.

Many players believe that they have climbed the mountain as soon as they have been picked for their country. It was never my intention to relax and be comfortable with that, for I always felt it was only the start, the bottom rung of the ladder. I remember play-ing in one match against the Rest of the World which quickly made me realise that I was not up there with the best of them. I therefore saw Scotland as the beginning and the training ground for bigger and better things. I was perhaps lucky that this presence of mind, discipline, dedication and ambition to push myself forward was part of my nature.

In the early days, the Scottish coaches were Derrick Grant and Ian McGeechan, and Ian continued as coach throughout my career. We went through my first three seasons with varying degrees of success. In 1987, we beat Ireland and Wales at Murrayfield and went to Twickenham with the chance of the Triple Crown. Originally we should have played England first up but, in a dreadful winter, the game was postponed and the match switched to much later in the season. That was a pity, because at the beginning England were in some disarray. However, by the time we came to play them on 4 April, they had got their act together and our hopes for a Triple Crown were savaged. We played abominably that day – it was probably one of the worst Scottish performances I was ever associated with. To rub salt into the wound, it was England's only win of the season, and they shared the Wooden Spoon with Wales.

Had we won the Triple Crown, it would have made all the difference, for it would have given our mental state a tremendous boost preparatory to going to New Zealand for the 1987 World

Cup. As it turned out, we performed competently enough to get to the quarter finals, where New Zealand, who were probably the best rugby side that I have ever played against and a team of immense talent, beat us heavily by 30–3.

I decided to stay on in New Zealand and play for Auckland Varsity, where I was lucky to play with Grant Fox, David Kirk, John Drake and Sean Fitzpatrick, all influential members of the All Blacks who had won the World Cup. We won the big league competition, the Gallacher Shield in Auckland, with a very strong side and I enjoyed the opportunity to experience the life of a New Zealander. I did not play Provincial rugby, but I sat on the bench for Auckland during a couple of matches. I understood that it was only my second year of International rugby and I learned so much playing with Grant Fox. Above all, I realised what a disciplinarian and how dedicated he was. He just took hold of the training session by going through all the moves with his fellow backs and was as strict as hell. If anyone dropped a pass, he wanted to know why, whether the pass was behind him, if it was a bad pass, or just carelessness. I think a lot of that experience rubbed off on me and I was quick to realise that, compared with our training at home, they were far more disciplined, while we were too relaxed and not hard enough on ourselves if we made mistakes.

I learned, above all, about the New Zealand compulsion and insistence on concentrating for every second. I discovered that practice makes perfect and you will only get from the game situation what you have done on the training field. If you are mucking around in practice, then you have no right to expect to perform at a high level in the match situation. For the next few years the Scottish players and the team began to take this on board and, from there on, learnt to play a lot harder and with more discipline than most other teams at that time.

Scotland continued, therefore, to survive with limited resources. Jim Telfer has always said that the Scottish players and the Scotland team have to work twice as hard and more strenuously than any other of the major Unions in the world, simply to keep pace with the rest. We recognise that we have limited player resources and, therefore, we try and ensure that everything we do is up to standard and that everyone is totally comfortable with the idea that we have to work harder to exist at the top level. There is no room for any grey area and it means that the sum of the whole must be greater than the sum of the individual parts, which is very true of the Scottish team. Collectively, we have been a very competitive side throughout the Eighties and early Nineties. In the early Eighties, standards were set by fine players like Colin Deans, Alan Tomes, Ian Milne, John Beattie, Iain Paxton, Jim Calder, David Leslie, Roy Laidlaw, John Rutherford, Andy Irvine, Bruce Hay, Jim Renwick and Roger Baird. Then, later into the Eighties, came another group of splendid players, like Finlay Calder, John Jeffrey, Derek White, David Sole, Scott Hastings and Iwan Tukalo, all of them tremendous ambassadors for Scottish and British rugby, and latterly Gary Armstrong, Craig Chalmers, Tony Stanger and Sean Lineen, and forwards such as Kenny Milne, Paul Burnell and Damian Cronin. For everything they achieved, they had to put in a hell of a lot of hard work, preparation, discipline and dedication; but also much of what they achieved came from the pride and the passion generated with the pulling on of the Scottish jersey with its thistle emblem. That is a tremendous feeling and there is also an element of vanity – perhaps one of the prime motivations of wanting to play for your country – which in its wake brings you so much fun and so many satisfying and fulfilling moments.

In the season preceding our second Grand Slam in six years and only our third ever, 1990, the writing was on the wall regarding our improvement. Under Finlay Calder, an inspirational captain, and with a new, young half back partnership in Gary Armstrong and Craig Chalmers, Scotland finished joint runners up after scoring their biggest home win against Wales; a 12–12 draw at Twickenham; and Scotland's highest ever score against any International Board country in beating Ireland 37–21 at Murrayfield. The latter was a terrific match in which the Irish, in their delightful manner, contributed as much to the enjoyment as we did. Paris continued to be our *bête noir*, for we have not won there since 1969, and again we lost 19–3.

The English, from the summer of 1989, when many of them had come back hardened after the Lions Tour of Australia, where their forwards had fought fierce battles with the Australian pack and learned some hard lessons, were also beginning to understand that they had great potential and were capable of doing something really big. They came back into the Five Nations in 1990 and hammered the three teams they encountered before coming to Murrayfield; beating Ireland 23–0, France 26–7, and Wales 34–6. In the meantime, Scotland achieved scratchy victories against Ireland and Wales but a substantial 21–0 win over France. Perhaps, therefore, the English could be forgiven for believing that they only had to turn up to win. They had scored some glorious tries throughout the championship by spinning the ball wide and they were just cruising along until they underestimated Scotland, and that is something you can never do.

I think the crucial English error was to listen to their own Press, something which has always been one of their fatal instincts. (Remember the World Cup Final of 1991!) I will never blame the English players for the way they performed, but I would blame the Press for hyping them up to such an extent that they were over-confident. They were all saying that they did not believe what the papers were saying, but subconsciously they must have felt that victory was theirs. They forgot that there were another 15 men wanting to do the same thing, with the tremendous advantage of the passion of the Murrayfield crowd, a key factor, and they also forgot Scottish pride, which simply would not allow our team to be squashed.

I remember a feeling of total confidence building up to the game and it did not even enter my head that we would lose. I think everyone involved that day thought the same and I can honestly say that I have never been as confident as I felt about beating England that day. Everyone said that our captain, David Sole, leading us out at a slow march on to the field was the greatest piece of psychology ever seen on a rugby field. It came out of a general discussion and we all said we would walk instead of trot out on to the field. We were so psyched up that the walk allowed us the opportunity to soak up the atmosphere from the hugely partisan Scottish crowd. A slow walk all the way down the tunnel to the 15-yard line is a hell of a long walk and it seemed like an eternity. I am not sure whose idea it was, but I think it was a collective decision by both the backs and the forwards, with Ian McGeechan and Jim Telfer also involved. I actually wanted to run on wearing our kilts, with shorts underneath, and we talked about a piper leading us on to the field, but we eventually decided that we would simply walk on at a measured pace.

England were ridiculous odds-on favourites for the match. It turned out not to be a thrilling game but it was exciting simply because it was so close and because of the intensity. It was certainly no classic, in any sense of the word, but that day Scotland played with such fervour that we reduced England, I believe, to a bunch of nervous wrecks. We, too, had learned on the back of the 1989 Lions Tour. The feeling of the Scottish camp was that we had learned just as much, if not more, than the England players from that experience and, as it proved, it stood us in better stead.

In Edinburgh the next day there was a headline which read, 'Bannockburn 13–14, Grand Slam 13–7.' I kept it, because it was so appropriate and obviously it was one of the greatest days in Scottish sporting history. No matter what happens in the future, that occasion took rugby in Scotland into a new era of media attention, for we took the full focus of the British Press for over a week.

I think that when we walked past the television cameras there was a terrible look on our faces and everyone watching at home realised there was mirrored an immense sense of determination and purpose. We all felt that it was the hardest game we ever had to play, because it had only happened once before that both England and Scotland were playing for the Grand Slam in the final game of the Five Nations Tournament. It was certainly the most hyped game in the history of the Calcutta Cup, as all the coveted trophies, including the Triple Crown and the Grand Slam, were at stake. The atmosphere at Murrayfield was electric as Scotland took all the prizes with a no-nonsense performance. Craig Chalmers kicked Scotland into a 6–0 lead in the first ten minutes, due to some indiscipline by the England pack. Guscott then dummied his way over for a try and a third penalty by Chalmers made it 9–4 at half-time. I was happy to be involved in creating a try soon after half-time, when I chipped ahead for Tony Stanger to score. A penalty by Hodgkinson was England's only riposte, for they never imposed themselves, and, by running kickable penalties, questions were raised after the match as to who was making the decisions on the pitch.

It was a huge body blow for England, but they put it behind them to achieve two back-to-back Grand Slams in the ensuing years. I will always believe that England started to get things right on the field because of one man – Ian McGeechan. Geoff Cooke was not the man who started that revolution because, in my opinion, he is a man manager, and a very good one, but not a coach of rugby players. I am firmly of the opinion that it was Ian McGeechan who was responsible for the resurgence of English rugby after the 1989 Lions Tour. Ask Brian Moore to put his hand on his heart and I am sure he would tell you exactly the same thing. Geoff Cooke got things right for England off the field by supplying all the support that is required for a national team, but they got things right on the field as well. Suddenly they were focused and organised. Look at Rob Andrew; Rob was a fairly average International rugby player until he came on the 1989

Lions Tour as a replacement and, since then, because of the influence of Ian McGeechan, he has become one of the best stand offs
in the world. His kicking has been precisely accurate and he is a
brave rugby player and a marvellous competitor.

I could never understand what all the controversy was about
concerning the contrasting attributes of Rob Andrew and Stuart
Barnes. In my opinion, there was no doubt that Rob was by far the
more potent and effective player. Although he proved the point
against Romania, France, Australia, New Zealand and then
reached a crescendo against South Africa in the Pretoria Test in the
summer of 1994, when he broke all the existing English scoring
records, time and again the English Press insisted on re-opening
the debate. On the Lions tour of 1993 there was no question and,
on merit, we picked Rob Andrew for all the Tests.

The English have claimed that since that climactic day in 1990
when they lost the Grand Slam the atmosphere between themselves and the Scots has changed dramatically. They feel that there
was animosity from the Scottish crowd and I can understand that.
The spectators were at fever pitch because of the intensity of the
game. Some 55,000 out of the 60,000 present were our supporters
and they were certainly not going to sit in their seats clapping
every good thing that England did. I think the English interpreted
the partisan and vigorous support from the crowd as being a hostile atmosphere. They were over-sensitive, for the Scottish crowd
is no more unsympathetic than the English supporters are towards
the Scottish team at Twickenham. Why is it that the English
always accuse the opposition of being the baddies and see themselves as the goodies? I think that England should occasionally
take a long, hard look at themselves and realise that they, too, are
far from perfect. I would refute all those allegations and just say
that there is nothing wrong with tremendous support received by
the opposition on their own ground. If Edinburgh is a bleak place
for England to play rugby, then that is fine by me. There are
plenty of other disagreeable places to play rugby and I have
played in many of them – none of them more uncomfortable than
Twickenham.

I certainly have no antipathy for members of the England
team and I have a great deal of respect for many of them, in particular men like Rob Andrew, Mike Teague, Dean Richards, Jason
Leonard and Brian Moore, Jerry Guscott, Dewi Morris, Peter
Winterbottom, and many others. As I have often said, friendship
only evolves once you have finished playing rugby and, because

of the intensity of International competition, it is not possible to sit down and say, 'You are a good friend of mine.' I think that can only be derived from mutual respect of each other and then, once your playing days are over, you can look back and say, 'Well, we had some great times. Let us forget the hostility of contest and conflict and become good friends.'

People often ask me whether there is an indifference between myself and Will Carling, and point out that he never said much about me that was friendly in his book. Well, that was up to him, but I really have no ill feeling towards him. Will is a very high-profile and talented player and I have respect for him as such.

People forget the good times. I recollect when the English and Scottish players were partners in crime and nicked the Calcutta Cup from the after-match dinner, and proceeded to turn it into a plate by kicking it down the Royal Mile, after showing it a few of the night spots of Edinburgh. It was a *cause celebre* at the time and the interesting thing was that, although it was basically an English possession, it was a Scottish player who was punished most severely, as John Jeffrey was banned from playing for a while, while Dean Richards merely got away with a caution.

The Calcutta Rugby Club, which disbanded in 1877 because the rapid development of polo provided a fatal blow to football, bequeathed the silver rupees left in the club kitty, amounting to 60 pounds sterling, to be made into a trophy of Indian workmanship and presented it to the RFU as an International Challenge Cup, to be played for annually by England and Scotland. It was first played for in 1878 and the dates of every match, with the name of the winning country and the names of the two captains, are recorded around the base. Considering that England, for security reasons, hold the Cup in a London vault, I thought they were pretty decent about the whole affair.

In the wider sense, Scottish rugby mid-1994 was at a cross-roads. Everyone recognised that there is a huge gulf between club and International rugby in Scotland, and that something has to be done to fill that gap in order to improve the fortunes of the International player in his preparation for a big game. You simply cannot expect men to be playing mediocre rugby one weekend and then to perform at International level the next. The divide is too immense. The Scottish Rugby Union, the players, the coaches, and even the smallest rugby clubs recognise this fact.

What needs to be done is the putting in place of a process whereby this big gap is reduced. It is my belief that this can only be achieved by playing more games at a District level, which would be a sort of equivalent of the Provincial level in New Zealand, Australia and South Africa. Our District teams, the South, Edinburgh, Glasgow, and the North and Midlands, are only barely comparable with club sides such as Leicester, Bath, Gloucester, Swansea, or Cardiff. At the moment, there are eight clubs in the first division of the Scottish League from Edinburgh. If these clubs act as feeder teams, then automatically the standard of rugby that is going to be played by the Edinburgh District team will be far higher, by virtue of the players selected being the best in their positions from all eight clubs.

If we achieve that, our aim must then be to find teams to play against. However, the Scottish Rugby Union are currently saying 'No' to such a scheme, and we have a first division of 14 teams from which the majority of players for Scotland are picked. One or two play in the second division, Andy Nicol and Alan Watt, which is quite ridiculous. What the SRU have agreed is that, from season 1995/96, the number of sides in the first division will be reduced to eight, each playing on a home and away basis and, as a result, the standard of rugby, in this division, will get higher and higher. I do not believe that, because what you are actually going to get is eight club sides attracting all the best players. If each club has, say, a squad of 20 players, that makes 160 players and I doubt that there are that many players remotely good enough to play for Scotland. Therefore, the standard is not going to rise sufficiently for those players who are good enough for International rugby to be adequately prepared for the huge rise in quality required for a Test match. Furthermore, it is likely that the majority of these top eight clubs will come from Edinburgh and the Borders, thus limiting the opportunities available for top-class rugby in Glasgow and Central Scotland.

I believe that there are only 40 or 50 players who are good enough, even in their wildest dreams, to be considered to represent Scotland or the Scotland 'A' side. Therefore, the South of Scotland, Edinburgh and Glasgow teams must find a high enough level to play at. At the moment we have a joint competition with the Irish Provincial sides, Munster, Leinster, Connaught and Ulster, but I believe that the only way forward is to encourage the formation of a British League, where you have the top teams in the British Isles competing. The top English and the Welsh club sides are not true club teams, for they draw from huge catchment areas and are more equivalent to the Provincial sides of the southern hemisphere. They all have their feeder clubs and, because there are only ten clubs in the English first division, all the major players in England have graduated largely to those top clubs. The only exception I can think of is Wade Dooley, who astonishingly played for Preston Grasshoppers in the fourth division. The likelihood of that situation happening again, however, is remote.

In Scotland we have but a tenth of the English resources. We can distil that into, say, three major teams; as I have already said, England have the ten club sides to which top players have graduated; Wales have between four and six top clubs which are creaming off the best Welsh players; and you have the four Irish Provincial sides. We could form these teams into a British Isles League, probably in two divisions. The problem would be the original seeding, but they would quickly find their level, and the end result would be a British Isles League to compare with the Currie Cup in South Africa and the Provincial Championship in New Zealand. In the end, you may have three divisions of the British League and then, below that, in Scotland and Ireland a district league, and in England and Wales two first divisions, all of which would be tied into a promotion and relegation system.

I believe that there is too much appalling parochialism in British rugby and I honestly think that, with both the English and Welsh clubs only playing against each other in their own environments, these insular and incestuous patterns could cause the sort of damage usually engendered by inbreeding. Instead, my system would ensure mini-International-type matches, which would generate huge interest, and we would be able to develop our rugby far more by feeding off each other. That could only happen if we are broad-minded enough and I do not know if the English are, but certainly the Welsh would be, and so would the Irish and the Scots.

It is apparent that England believe they are so powerful now that they do not want the Welsh clubs to get strong by playing them, for Twickenham recently poured cold water on the idea of an Anglo-Welsh League, even though most of their first-class clubs approved and met the Welsh at Tewkesbury early in the season to discuss the matter. Some Englishmen were even saying at the start of the 1994 season that they might drop the Celtic sides and the Five Nations Tournament, which would be insane. I know that, at the moment, England are not going to learn much from us, but times have a habit of changing. After all, Scotland should have beaten them in 1994, Wales beat them in 1993 and Ireland beat them home and away in those two years. Now, if England want to go and do their own thing then that is fine. I do not really give a damn, but I think it is they who will suffer in the long run.

The Scottish Rugby Union's idea of an eight-club league is going to put more pressure on the top players, but I repeat that I do not believe that these club matches will be of a sufficiently high level to raise standards, and in Scotland there is an urgent need to cut out the Mickey Mouse games.

Many believe that two Grand Slams in 1984 and 1990 were due to the fact that we were the first people to introduce leagues and organise competitive rugby in the British Isles. I do not subscribe to that theory, and I actually think that it was in spite of the system that we achieved such success. I honestly believe that it was due to the arrival of some very talented players throughout the Eighties, and also because we had some great leaders. Look at the people who captained Scotland in that era. Jim Aitken was a terrific captain in 1984, a hugely inspirational guy. He was followed by Colin Deans, who was a world-class hooker and who should have been the first choice for the 1983 Lions, when they appointed the Irishman Ciaran Fitzgerald as captain. Next came Gary Callander, another tremendous rugby player, not so well known because he played only a short time, and he sat on the bench a record number of times as reserve to Colin Deans. He was followed by the strong hard man, Finlay Calder, who led the Lions in a winning Test series, and finally David Sole. If David had not retired in 1992 then, without question, he would have led the 1993 Lions. I then took over from David as the Scottish skipper and also captained the Lions, which I think establishes my credentials.

In addition, you have to look at the coaches of that period. There was Derrick Grant, who was a widely respected coach, and then you had Jim Telfer and Ian McGeechan, who both coached the British Lions, with the latter being the only man to have coached them on two tours. We have, therefore, had an amazing group of people at the helm, who guided Scotland through the most fruitful era in their history. Scotland grasped the idea that we had to work extremely hard earlier than the other home nations, but I suppose that the new leagues did help in the identification of our best players.

Another magnificent milestone by the Scottish Rugby Union came when they took the decision to go ahead with the complete redevelopment of Murrayfield, following the Taylor Report. The stadium is now the most modern in Britain, soccer or rugby, and a tremendous testament to the forward thinking and management skills of the SRU. They were very bold and their timing was exceptional, for it was launched just prior to the World Cup, with Scotland playing all their matches at Murrayfield. The depth of support and the feeling that resulted because of the performance of the Scottish side provided a splendid launch pad for the whole marketing campaign. The ground was also rebuilt on the back of Scotland having a very good record in the Five Nations Championship at Murrayfield, with their supporters coming to see some spectacular games full of drama, suspense and excitement.

I think we can congratulate all the committee who made the decision, especially Bill Hogg, the Chief Executive of the SRU, who is a long-time administrator there and who was wise enough to understand the requirement of high standards of safety and comfort needed for rugby's new age; together with other people like Duncan Paterson, the Chairman of Selectors and manager of the Scotland team in the 1991 World Cup, Bob Munro, World Cup manager in 1987, and Fred McLeod, the current Treasurer of the International Board. All these men have had a long involvement on the committees of Scottish rugby and they can bask in the pleasure of seeing the benefits of this fabulous new stadium. The secret now is to get the stadium used more often and we should see a number of interesting new concepts coming through.

I suppose the SRU Committee has, in the past, had the reputation of being one of the most conservative and remote bodies in the rugby world. This is no longer true, as we have recently seen with their radical idea of experimenting with the laws of the game and even reducing the number of players to 13, as in Rugby League.

Much has been written concerning the sterility of the 1993/94 season, when the Five Nations Tournament produced only 20 tries to 61 penalty goals, and particularly about the crowding of play in midfield causing such traffic jams that scoring tries became a rarity. I believe that the points raised by the Scottish Union are all very valid and, if you were to reduce the numbers to 13 players, you would certainly have more space in which to operate the ball, which, after all, is what rugby is designed for. If the two flankers go, is the scrummage going to retain the dominance that it now has, and are you going to retain the traditionally shaped prop or would you, in effect, move two flanker-type players to the prop position and just use the scrums as a means of restarting the game? In other words, are we moving away from the old tradition that rugby is a game for people of all shapes and sizes?

England have always been comforted by the realisation that their players can always adapt and play within the laws, but, strangely, they are the first ones to complain when the laws are changed, because it requires the coaches and the players to think deeply about the changing style of the game. They were lucky that the new ruck and maul laws played right into their hands because, as a general rule, they possess far bigger men than Ireland, Scotland and Wales.

I am convinced that there is a role in modern rugby for a very creative and innovative coach, who could introduce new ideas. Who says that the scrum half has got to be a slight guy with quickness of foot and a tremendous pass? Why not redefine the role? Gary Armstrong plays a vastly different type of game at scrum half than does someone like David Kirk or Robert Jones, both wonderful scrum halves. Gary Armstrong is an absolute menace on the rugby field in a physical way that Robert Jones could never be, but Robert is a menace in different ways, with his beautifully long accurate service and telling kicks. Gary is a real terrier in the way that he goes charging into the opposition back rows.

I think people underestimate the complexity and the intellectuality of Rugby Football, and these new ideas are all very well and extremely interesting, but it remains to be seen whether the experiments will work, and then if any other countries will back the Scottish Rugby Union.

We must recognise that the game has changed dramatically and we now have to look at ways of making it more of a spectacle for the paying supporters, who at the moment are being served poor fare, and a greater joy for the player. At least the Scottish Rugby Union cannot be accused of sitting on their backsides and doing nothing. I discuss the laws and the evolution of the game elsewhere in more detail.

We, the players, have in fact built up an excellent rapport with our Union and I would congratulate them for listening to the players and understanding that, when the International Rugby Board's regulations on amateurism opened up, change was inevitable. Consequently, the Scottish players have got it entirely right, because we were prepared to go along with the Union and wait until they were satisfied that what they were doing was within the regulations laid down by the International Board. There is no animosity between us and the Committee, largely because we did not go and shoot our mouths off like some of the English players.

They showed their appreciation of our tact by being supportive of us, and they demonstrated considerable initiative by ensuring that we were the first northern hemisphere side to have a team sponsor, The Famous Grouse, a great whisky to the uninitiated. By and large they have got things right and I am pleased with the way things have progressed. I wanted to be sure, given my relationship with the Union, which has been a good one at all times, that the process was in place for future players to be beneficiaries of something that we current players had negotiated. You can always look for improvement, but I have little criticism of the Union.

The SRU have put an operation into progress whereby we, the players, have been able to have a number of sponsors. Some of the Union sponsors have come in and allocated a portion of the money, or some extra money, into the players' kitty. This is administered by Ian McLauchlan, that great prop forward for Scotland and the British Lions, known as Mighty Mouse. Generally, we are rewarded for personal appearances and endorsements of the sponsors' products and doing public relations, which are within the IRB regulations. It is not an awful lot of money, but, having said that, it is certainly helpful to some of the students in the squad. We are still trying to establish when the payments should be made to individuals, but at least we know where it is coming from and where it is going, and I think it is fairly easy to administer in a country as small as Scotland.

We do not have trust funds for players, but I think it is something that we must look at, and for someone like myself, who does not necessarily need a couple of thousand pounds at this stage of my life, it would be better if that money was put away in a tax-efficient, high-return investment which will be of more use to me in a number of years rather than at present. There are steps afoot to look at this and what else needs to be done, but until there is substantial money available the whole exercise tends to be hypothetical.

At this point, and for the record, the Scottish team that I would most like to play in would comprise David Sole, Colin Deans, Ian Milne, Chris Gray, Alan Tomes, John Jeffrey and Finlay Calder; John Beattie, Gary Armstrong and John Rutherford; with Iwan Tukalo, Jim Renwick, Scott Hastings and Keith Robertson on the right wing. That is a team I would have loved to see in the Scottish jersey, all at the same time. It would, at each player's peak, have power, pace, aggression, skill and artistry, and great

64

strength all the way through the forwards and backs. I realise, of course, that such a choice is very subjective and that other people will have their own views, but I feel I must put my head on the block and say it, so that I am not put on the spot in the future. It would be interesting to see how that team compares with those picked by my contemporaries.

CHAPTER V

An Antipodean Brainwave

THE FIRST EVER Rugby World Cup, which projected the game into the 20th century, very nearly did not happen, as the barriers put up against the concept were considerable. We now tend to forget that the four Home Nations were, in the end, dragged kicking and screaming into the tournament by its true creators, Australia and New Zealand. A major problem was the question of sponsorship and it was not until very late in the day, when the objections of Japan against the breaching of amateur regulations were satisfied, that the principal sponsor, KDD, was finally enrolled and, to the great relief of Australia and New Zealand, the competition proceeded. It was probably the greatest single step the game had taken in its history and the ramifications are still being felt and evaluated.

Strangely, the inaugural World Cup was never properly chronicled, apart from a publication in the Welsh language by Thomas Davies, BBC Wales' radio sports producer and a great follower and enthusiast of the game. Nevertheless, this first World Cup was one of the big milestones in the development of our winter game, which is now played in over 140 countries. It was a triumph for those people in Australia and New Zealand who created the idea and then implemented it against considerable opposition, some of it savage, particularly from those conservative Unions of the four Home Countries.

They all feared that the competition would apply undue pressures and professional attitudes, thus destroying the amateur ethos of the game. Such horrors and pessimism were proved to be without foundation, and the Cup became a remarkable, runaway success, not only in producing excellent rugby and memorable games, but also in helping the administrators, at the time, to re-establish their control over the amateur values of the game. The game's administrators were out to show that those virtues of high principles and moral standards, without which the amateur game might die, could survive even at the highest level of competition. I always believed that such a competition would raise the game to its proper place in the public eye, as the second most important world-wide winter game – a position which, strangely enough, it had never before fully attained.

The first rugby World Cup was also the saviour of the International Rugby Football Board, whose influence was in con-siderable decline. Not only did the World Cup become a vehicle by which the Board could become relatively self-financing, from an income derived from its subsidiary company, Rugby World Cup Incorporated, but it also helped to fend off the growing challenge of the French dominated FIRA (Federation Internationale de Rugby Amateur), which presented an increasing attraction because of the dissatisfaction of major southern hemisphere coun-tries, together with that of emerging nations, such as America and Canada, believing, as they did, that the French-led organisation in continental Europe was a more progressive body. The whip-hand held by the IRFB, at the time, was that the first World Cup was by invitation only. Even now it is only open to member countries of the IRFB, which has developed into a major organisation of over 60 members and is still growing, with new, impressive head-quarters in Bristol in the UK. They have controlled the qualifying rounds that have now been played all over the world for the 1995 World Cup in South Africa.

It was only the grim persistence of Australia and New Zealand which brought their brainchild to fruition. These Unions, Australia in particular, have traditionally both been far more *avant garde* than our Home Unions. Once again they were right, for they understood that if Rugby Football was to continue its worldwide evolution and development, then it required a showpiece and shop window such as the Rugby World Cup.

The World Cup just sort of arrived as far as we players were concerned, and no one quite knew what we were going into at that stage. It was such an exhilarating and exciting idea for us, and we Scots, of course, wanted to ensure that Scotland would not only be well represented but that we should try and win the tournament, which would have been a terrific coup for a nation with such limited resources. We knew that many of our Scottish ancestors went to New Zealand and that we would get a considerable following and, therefore, we were delighted to be seeded in one of the three pools in that country, with France, Romania and Zimbabwe, and not in the one pool in Australia, which consisted of Australia, England, USA and Japan.

We arrived in New Zealand after the most horrific journey, with stops at Dubai and Singapore. On the same flight as the Welsh and Irish teams we discovered that they were just as excited and just as much in the dark as to what to expect. Our first problem came when we were about to touch down in Auckland and a huge bank of cloud enveloped the airport, so we zoomed off again and were taken all the way down to Christchurch, in the South Island, where we sat on the runway for an hour and a half before returning to Auckland. When we arrived at our base camp, the Hyatt Hotel, the Irish and Welsh players decided to relax, but Scotland, in their wisdom, decided to go out and have a training session. When you have been on a plane for over 30 hours you become a bit pent up with frustration and, although we were only supposed to be playing a light game of touch rugby, it suddenly developed into a full-blown physical game.

On reflection, it was ridiculous that we should train with such intensity for an hour and a half, having just stepped off the plane. The following day Derrick Grant, our very ruthless coach from Hawick, decided that we would have a scrummaging session against Ireland at the Grammar Club in Auckland, for which the Whetton brothers play. It was a gorgeous day, and immediately the two sets of forwards were knocking hell out of each other, literally within 20 hours of arriving. Both countries, wishing to leave nothing to chance, were taking their preparation too seriously. We had been out for a three-hour session and in the last five minutes my brother Scott pulled his hamstring which put him out of the World Cup. He played very briefly for a few seconds against Romania but failed to overcome the damage done at that too rigorous early session. The whole attitude towards training and travelling has changed dramatically from those days, but then you live and learn.

The first couple of days was spent in Auckland, in lovely weather, and there was a gala inaugural dinner for the 12 teams based in New Zealand, while the four sides in Australia had their own dinner in Sydney. To meet 12 teams from all over the world at one function was an unusual experience, and that was the moment when everybody recognised that we were entering into something very new and tremendously exciting. It was to begin the process of a considerable interchange of ideas between players from different cultures regarding the course that we wanted the game to take in the years ahead. The whole of the New Zealand rugby public were as excited and enthralled as we were at the prospect of playing a World Cup, but as it was only my second year in International rugby, no one was more excited than I.

From Auckland we flew down to Christchurch on the Canterbury Plain, where we basically took over the whole of the Hornby Trust Hotel. They were amazingly hospitable and kind to us and, with their eager co-operation, we had some delightful parties. Hornby is a suburb of Christchurch and we used to go training at the Hornby Rugby Club, just along the road from the hotel. We settled in comfortably. Our opening match was at one of New Zealand's traditional Test match venues, Lancaster Park in Christchurch, against France, and it was probably one of the most dramatic games of the whole World Cup. Scotland played very, very well, and I remember hearing the pipe band playing out on the pitch. When you are a million miles away from home, to hear your own national instrument, the bagpipes, which are so synonymous with Scotland, is an inspiring experience.

We were splendidly supported by the South Island Scots, who we always felt would be on our side, and they were, particularly after Scotland played as well as they were capable of in their first match against the French. I remember Matt Duncan scoring a try right at the death of the 80 minutes, to bring the score level at 20–20, and I had a conversion on the right-hand touch line which, unhappily, just missed. We were not too despondent with a draw because we had played so well, and we felt that we could now win our other two games in the pool matches. I remember Blanco scoring a ridiculous try, when Berbizier, who was injured on the field, miraculously shuffled off it and Blanco, tapped the ball to himself and ran up the touch line, passing me, which he was more than capable of doing, and scored a try under the posts that really turned the game in their favour. It was a piece of Gallic gamesmanship which took us all by surprise, but it made us bloody angry, so we came storming back with that final score.

Who would have thought that the first match of Pool 4 could have rekindled the excitement and the passion of our recent meet-

70

ing at Parc des Princes in the Five Nations Championship, when France won a dramatic game by 28–22, and also it lit a touchpaper for an explosive example of fine attacking play to launch the inaugural World Cup? The Scottish performance was all the more commendable because we lost our most important figure, the world class outside half, John Rutherford, with a knee injury, only seven minutes after the start. This only served to act as a goad to the remarkable impetus and effort of the Scottish back row of Finlay Calder, Iain Paxton and John Jeffrey, who played out of their skins.

This had been the first day of the tournament proper, 23 May, when England also played Australia, two matches of such high drama, controversy, suspense and skill, which gave the tournament a tremendous kick start and made everyone realise that the World Cup was going to be a marvellous success. The remaining matches in our pool then became a formality, though Zimbabwe had their finest moment in losing by a single point to Romania.

We played Zimbabwe next, at Athletic Park, Wellington, a game we won easily by 60-21. We scored 11 tries that day and no penalty goals, but I got a record of eight conversions to add to a try, so I thoroughly enjoyed that. We then had to play our third game in eight days, against Romania in Dunedin, which is the Edinburgh of the southern hemisphere, and we realised that, whatever happened, we really had to win this game. We approached it with tremendous intensity and were rewarded with another big win of 55–28. I had the satisfaction of beating the world record at the time, by scoring 27 points, with two tries, one penalty and eight conversions. My record was one of the shortest lived in rugby history, for Didier Camberabero surpassed it two hours later, against Zimbabwe at Eden Park, with 30 points from three tries and nine conversions.

I remember when Scotland played Zimbabwe in the second game of the World Cup and Colin Deans, our captain, won his 50th cap. We came back into the changing-room and we were pretty euphoric, after an extremely easy victory. We had played exceptionally well and we knew we were going to have a few jars in celebration. Roy Laidlaw, that great Scottish half back and a lovely guy, went on to make a wonderful speech about Colin's contribution to Scottish Rugby. He said he would like to present Colin with a small memento on behalf of the team. We all then looked around and realised that Colin was not in the changing-room, as he was giving a television interview out in the warm-up room, as he was giving a television interview out in the warm-up area. It was absolutely hilarious, because Roy had really put a lot of work into making his speech. When we realised that Roy had not struck home, because Colin was not there, and therefore had to do it all over again, we all fell about laughing.

We now knew that we were going to play New Zealand in the quarter finals of the World Cup and that it was going to be a completely different kettle of fish, for they had scored 70 points in their opening game against Italy, 74 against Fiji and a mere 46 against Argentina. However, I think they, too, recognised that Scotland would provide them with a much sterner challenge in the first knockout stage of the cup.

I will always remember lining up next to the All Blacks in the tunnel at Lancaster Park, just prior to running out onto the field. The All Blacks were in the white jerseys which they only ever wear when they play against Scotland at home. Even in virginal white they looked awesome and forbidding and so much bigger than the Scotland team. We went out and gave it our best shot, but we were no match for them and they won 30–3. Although they only scored two tries, I came off after the game thinking that we got positively and unequivocally hammered. Never, in my two years of playing International rugby up until then, had I realised that there could be such a gulf between us and any team, because I always felt that we could be entirely competitive against anybody. I discovered how wrong I was. They were built differently, more experienced and played at a different pace, and the game was far more physical than we expected. As Derrick Grant said in the Press conference afterwards, when he was asked what he thought of New Zealand, 'They simply breed a different kind of animal.'

I do not think Scotland let themselves down. We only lost one game against the ultimate winners, merely conceding two tries, and if we were well beaten by New Zealand, then so was everybody else, with Wales, who came third in the tournament after beating Australia in Rotorua, losing to them 49–6 in the semi-final and France 29–9 in the final. Playing against the World Champions was invaluable experience for both me and the Scottish team. It was my early days in the game, and it set me targets to aim at, difficult as they were. I think, at that stage, New Zealand were so far ahead of the rest of the rugby-playing countries of the world that they would have walked the World Cup against a combination of all the best players from the other countries. They were that good, so much fitter and technically more advanced than the rest of us. Above all, they showed the rest of the world how to launch damaging attacks off the back of the scrum, using that redoubtable back row trio – Buck Shelford, Alan Whetton and Michael Jones.

As I have said, it was a great forum for all the players of the world to get together and unite. Many of us had never been to New Zealand before although we knew that rugby was their religion, which they lived and breathed, week in week out. We arrived and, switching on the television, we saw a commercial featuring Andy Dalton, the All Black hooker and captain for the World Cup, who never played in any of the games. Andy was appearing in a TV commercial for a tractor and he said, 'I am Andy Dalton, a farmer', but everyone in New Zealand also knew full well that Andy Dalton was more than that, he was a famed captain of the All Blacks and to us it appeared that he was driving a huge articulated lorry through the International Board Regulations. We also saw other players like John Kirwan endorsing products. We suddenly realised that this was a different situation, unheard of in the UK, and as conservative Scots we felt pretty strongly about this contravention of the amateur laws of rugby football; however, we recognised that New Zealand was a very different country and in retrospect we may have been a little naive.

Looking back now, there is no doubt this was our first indication that we were in a different ball game and perhaps signalled our first change of mood towards the relaxation of the amateur laws in the British Isles. It has been a potent factor for years in Australia and New Zealand, where they have been driving convoys of horses and carts through the amateur regulations. I suppose that we Europeans have always been totally artless in that regard, but then you only get your knowledge from visiting and living in other countries and experiencing their attitudes and cultures.

That apart, in my experience, the 1987 New Zealand side were probably one of the finest rugby sides that ever took the field, and only the 1971 and 1974 Lions and the 1984 and 1991 Wallabies can be talked of in the same breath. If, in their time, they were a class apart I do not think that they were ever as great a side again after that first World Cup. They seemed to peak for that occasion and were completely dynamic in everything they did. They were extraordinarily talented all the way through the team, and they were so far ahead of us in terms of their tactics and what they were trying to achieve on the rugby field, by playing total 15-man rugby.

One of the men of the tournament was Buck Shelford, who took the number eight position into a new dimension. I have never seen anything like the way he played off the back row of the scrum, where he was the sharp cutting edge of the All Blacks with his withering drives which unerringly broke the gain line. It often took four or five men to stop him. Then, when you consider the rest of the pack, with front row John Drake, Sean Fitzpatrick and Steve McDowell, second row Murray Pierce and Gary Whetton, and flankers Alan Whetton and Michael Jones, you realise what a dreadful handful they were to play against.

David Kirk, who took over the captaincy in the absence of Dalton, was not only highly intelligent and a very efficient scrum half and captain, but a marvellous catalyst to get things going, and the ideal link between forwards and backs. Grant Fox was the scoring machine. He scored the most points in the competition, 126 in five games, and his nearest competitor was Michael Lynagh with 82 points, whilst I came a poor third with 62. Smoking Jo Stanley and Warwick Taylor were the centres, John Kirwan and Craig Green the wings, and John Gallagher was the full back; a team which will go down as one of the very greatest in Rugby's Hall of Fame.

I am often asked what makes the All Blacks better than us. They are nearly the same size and do the same sort of jobs and bleed like the rest of us. I think that what makes them is the All Black history and tradition, which in their psyche provokes a real dread of losing. It is every young kid's dream to grow up and become an All Black; they are revered like film stars and are doted upon by the young women, so there is every incentive for rugby players in New Zealand to become an All Black, because of the high profile and the aura which surrounds them. If there are one hundred and twenty thousand players in New Zealand, then those who get to play for the All Blacks are going to be the very best. In contrast, there are only fourteen thousand players in Scotland and obviously the standard is not going to be as high.

I also think that their organisation and the back-up for the team, in terms of facilities and care, has always been better than anything we have achieved in Britain, until the very recent years. They have always had better structures right throughout the age groups in all the Provinces and they have been light years ahead of us in coaching. Their administrators appear more street-wise than ours and I recall the New Zealand Barbarians coming over to this country before the World Cup, when they blooded players such as Michael Jones, Alan Whetton and John Gallagher. They gave them a hard tour in the UK and all of a sudden we find these guys, a few months later, playing as well as any of the others in the Rugby World Cup Final. There are many reasons for the All Blacks having such a terrific record but it is part of the whole underlying way of life in New Zealand, where rugby is such a close-knit family community, which allows the teamwork and the coaching to come through. Everyone wants to play rugby. I believe it is as simple as that.

As I have said, I had the opportunity to stay in Auckland after the World Cup and to see just what makes the All Blacks tick, for I was between jobs and I had an offer to start in London with a firm of chartered surveyors, Richard Ellis, in January 1988. I felt it would be a good experience, but I was not sure where I was going to play. However, I was confident that, if I let enough people know during the World Cup, then something would turn up. So it did and although I had an opportunity to go down to Otago and perhaps play Provincial rugby, I was happy to end up playing club rugby for Auckland University. The Auckland Club Competition is extremely strong and very well organised. In fact, I only played seven games for Auckland University, including the Gallacher Shield final, when we beat Marist, who included in their ranks John Kirwan, Zinzan Brooke and Bernie McCahill from the All Blacks World Cup-winning squad. I really loved to see Zinzan play, for he is a terrific player and a marvellous athlete who became better and better as he got older.

I did feel, however, that in 1987, 1988 and 1989 they were perhaps a wee bit too serious about their rugby and did not know when to lighten up a little. I certainly believe that the All Blacks of 1993, when the Lions were out there, learned to smile a bit more and to be more people-friendly and less dour than the old-style All Blacks. They were less aloof and a far easier bunch to get on with, but they still had that incredible commitment and determination and were a magnificent team. I believe that when they had their worldwide dominance dented during the 1991 World Cup they learned to be more humble in defeat, which in turn made them more friendly.

In that time, since 1987, it is the Australians who have become much stronger as a Rugby Union nation. In many ways they have taken over the limelight from the All Blacks, but I think Australian rugby players have a strange arrogance, quite different from that of the All Blacks. Currently, Australia seem to have the greater competitive edge, that same sort of edge that the All Blacks always had over European teams.

I think that comes down to having marvellous coaches, in Bob Dwyer and Bob Templeton, a consistency in selection and, of course, some very talented players, including the present-day, absolute necessity of a huge pack of forwards, and especially powerful back row men such as Tim Gavin and Willy Ofahengaue. There is also no doubt in my mind that the Super-6, now superseded by the Super-10 Competition, benefited Australian rugby, because it exposed them to the harder, more physical side of New Zealand Rugby outside the Test matches. The Australians have been very quick learners and after hitting rock bottom in the late Seventies they became the most innovative and improved rugby nation on earth.

If we are going to compete, then we have to work as hard and follow the same weight and gymnasium programmes with equal commitment. I do not believe that British players follow programmes with the same dedication, for in the contemporary game it is still largely a matter of physical strength, particularly in the upper body. We are a long way behind Australia and New Zealand in this area. I also think that they have greater resolution, because there are greater rewards in the southern hemisphere and, therefore, a bigger incentive to win. I do not believe that their will to win is any stronger; it is simply that their climate allows them to put in much more effective work, and in Australia and New Zealand they are better organised and more geared up, because of their far better climatic conditions, towards increasing physical fitness. It is more scientific and properly controlled by bodies such as the Australian Institute of Sport, whereas we pretend that we know what we are doing but, in fact, we are only touching the surface and pretending that we are covering the ground.

This is a major failure of the game in Britain. We really have to look at the structure and design of our fitness programmes. I have no doubt that we lack the organisation and purpose on which the game is based in Australia and New Zealand. In Britain there is no real build-up to the Five Nations Championship, or to major tours. There is merely a hotch-potch of league games, whereas in Australia and New Zealand everything is far more geared towards improvement as the season goes on, thus giving them a better chance and a greater level of fitness once the bigger games arrive.

We had some marvellous times during the 1987 World Cup,

for I think that touring abroad brings a very special lifestyle. We thoroughly enjoyed each other's company. I think Scottish players are born tourists; perhaps that is why you find Scots all over the world, and, no matter where they go and what circumstances they are in, they certainly have their share of fun. We had some tremendous times at the Hornby Trust Hotel in Christchurch, and we used to invite our supporters along to join in the fun. After the games, especially the French match, and after the quarter final defeat against New Zealand, we had the most wonderful parties. That is part of rugby, putting your disappointments behind you and just getting on with enjoying yourselves, which we certainly did on those occasions.

That first World Cup brought it home to us what a tremendous opportunity and experience it was to learn about all the other countries of the world, by meeting their players and playing in the one country. We obviously received tremendous insights into training methods and different thinking, and the way that games were played overseas. You are a wee bit blinkered when you only play in the Five Nations without having the opportunity to tour. I remember when I first got capped for Scotland in 1986, we shared the Championship and then went down to Twickenham in 1987 for a chance of the Triple Crown, which we lost – nevertheless, we realised that we were more than capable of holding our own and doing well in the Five Nations. Then suddenly you go out and confront the likes of New Zealand and you are brought down to earth with a bump with the realisation that there is so much further to go, not only in terms of the playing standards of one's team, but in improving one's own individual performance.

There are two ways you can go about it. Either you realise that you are not prepared to offer the commitment and dedication required to have an even chance of beating the All Blacks, or else you decide that you can do something about it. I have always entirely supported the latter, for I feel that you are only given a brief opportunity to play rugby during a few short years, and, therefore, you must take advantage of that opportunity. I know no one can ever accuse me of not making the most of the chance, but then I have always enjoyed testing myself against the best, and certainly in 1987 the best in the world was New Zealand. I cannot understand those people who satisfy themselves with winning another cap, without doing full justice to that honour by giving their all on the field.

It would be remiss of me if I did not say that much of the

success of that inaugural World Cup was due to the marvellous hospitality of countless New Zealanders and Australians, who really put themselves out to give all the overseas players a good time. Furthermore, without that army of volunteer helpers, it could have been an absolute shambles instead of being an excellent prototype for the future evolution of the tournament.

Rugby is no different from the rest of the sporting world in terms of unpredictability and the sheer bloodymindedness that teams seem to acquire to make the odds look ridiculous. That first World Cup was, therefore, an opportunity for the minnows to have a go at the global giants of rugby, which at the time were the eight full International Board members. The only other world forum where the little guy can have a go at the big boys is the Hong Kong Sevens, which is comparable in standards of skill and fitness, but the rugby World Cup is the true stage and a far more serious and important matter.

Although there were some very heavy defeats, with Italy, Fiji and Zimbabwe conceding mammoth 70-point or more scores, and Japan 60, there were also some surprising results, with Fiji producing the biggest bombshell when they beat a seeded Argentina 28–9. Remarkably, Italy then beat Fiji 18–15, but Fiji advanced to the quarter finals because they scored the most tries in all the pool matches. Canada and Tonga gave both Ireland and Wales the fright of their lives. The Canadians led Wales 9–6 at half-time at Invercargill and, with quarter of an hour to go, were level with Ireland at 19–19, but ran out of steam late in both games. Although America got immense satisfaction from beating Japan, it was the Japanese, of all the unseeded sides, who perhaps gave the outstanding performance when, in the last match of the qualifying stages of the tournament, they led Australia 3–0, 9–4 and then 13–10. Very late in the game they missed a conversion which would have reduced the leeway to a mere goal away from the biggest upset in the history of rugby football. However, two late tries in injury time got Australia home more respectably than they deserved. It proved that even the giants have their bad games, and it is that glorious uncertainty which is another of the charms of a great game called Rugby Union Football.

CHAPTER VI

Campo's Cup

THE SECOND WORLD CUP, in 1991, was the biggest sporting event anywhere in the world that year, with the top 16 rugby playing countries gathering in the British Isles and France to play 32 matches in pursuit of the William Webb Ellis Cup. Over one million spectators saw the matches live, more than two billion people in 70 countries watched on television, and 40 countries took the live telecast of the final. It is, of course, television that makes it all a viable proposition and which, in turn, brings in the big sponsors. It was, nevertheless, a struggle for CPMA, the management company appointed by Rugby World Cup Inc, to find the necessary sponsorship due to the world business recession.

It was also the first time that a commercial television network had been awarded a major rugby contract in the British Isles. Previously, rugby football had been almost the private reserve of the BBC, whose obligation to, and presentation of, the Five Nations Tournament has always been first-class. On this occasion money talked and ITV Sport were awarded the contract as host broadcasters, together with TFI and Canal Plus in France, and RTE in Ireland. In the event, ITV showed a remarkable commitment to the tournament and as a consequence have again won the contract for 1995. They failed, however, in the Spring of 1994, to win the three-year Five Nations contract, which went to the BBC, but at a massively increased fee. Surprisingly, too, the Corporation have farmed out *Rugby Special* to an independent production company.

Happily, the tournament was once more a marvellous

occasion, full of many vivid matches, with those eight leading International Board countries, the big fish, all finding sharks in their pools. Suddenly emerging countries such as Canada and Western Samoa reached the quarter finals. Canada disposed of the more established countries, Fiji and Romania, and gave the French a tremendous run for their money in Agen, where they lost by a mere 19-13, but still qualified as runners-up in their pool and proceeded in the quarter final, on a water-logged pitch at Lille, to give the All Blacks a severe examination in strength and courage. Astonishingly, the Canadians were ten pounds heavier in the forwards than the All Blacks, and their sheer size and spirit produced a really tough and well-matched contest. It was only the streetwise use of the ball by the All Blacks which saw them through, and Canada even succeeded in scoring two tries against them.

The other huge surprise came when Western Samoa beat Wales, the top-seeded team in Pool 3 by virtue of coming third in the first World Cup, after beating Australia in the play-off. This was to cause great grief to the Welsh, for it meant that they now had to qualify for the finals of the 1995 World Cup, and were forced to play qualifying matches against Portugal in Lisbon and Spain in Madrid, which ultimately they won by mammoth scores. They then had to play Italy in Cardiff and Romania in Bucharest, in the autumn of 1994, to determine their pool in the World Cup.

It was all a bit absurd from the Welsh point of view, as the indignity was entirely due to a disputed try awarded by the French referee to Western Samoa when it was obvious to everybody else, and to the television cameras, that Robert Jones had got there first. It was the final Welsh denouement after a long period of decline which to some extent broke the heart of a proud rugby nation. Perhaps it became less hurtful when, in April 1994 in the Super-10 competition, the remarkable Western Samoans beat Auckland, who in turn had beaten my Lions side in 1993. However, Wales again became the Five Nations Champions in 1994 and it was obvious that they were on the way back. In the World Cup after next, there will only be three seeded teams and everybody else will have to qualify. I see such a process developing into the sort of farce imposed on Wales in Portugal, when, to the detriment of the Portuguese morale, they scored 102 points, unless Rugby World Cup sees to it that the qualifying games are, in turn, carefully seeded.

As in 1987, the 1991 World Cup was an outstanding success, but it was also seen by the media as a further and more definitive watershed than the first World Cup on the road to the game becoming professional. It was continuously examined as to whether commercialism would damage the spirit of the game and affect those Corinthian attitudes, which had seen it survive through thick and thin during its more muted amateur years. The debate between those who want to keep the amateur ethos pure, those who, at the very least, want rewards for loss of work and money, and others who are demanding flat-out professionalism, particularly in South Africa and New Zealand, is still unresolved. I cover these aspects elsewhere in this book.

There was some evidence in the 1991 World Cup that some of the lessons learned in the southern hemisphere tournament in 1987 had been digested, for England reached the final and Scotland the semis, so obviously there was considerable development by the northern hemisphere countries.

Another role of the World Cup is to propagate and popularise rugby worldwide and before the 1991 Tournament ended five more countries had applied to join the International Rugby Board to become part of the superb scene of rugby football.

There was, of course, a downside to the events, like the infamous Dubroca affair in Paris, when the New Zealand referee, David Bishop, was hassled and jostled in the tunnel after the England and France quarter final, as the immense disappointment just became too much for the Gallic temperament. Once the French were out of the competition, they lost all interest, evidenced by the fact that the next day, when New Zealand met Canada, they did not even bother to distribute the programmes, leaving them in bundles under the stand.

There were also flaws and inconsistencies in the refereeing, particularly with regard to players going to ground. Southern hemisphere referees had been refereeing that aspect of the ruck and maul pretty fiercely over a number of years, whereas the northern hemisphere had not been too fussy. The result was that there was a big clamp down after a referees meeting in Cardiff, where they were told by Roger Vanderfield to concentrate ruthlessly on this issue. Subsequently, we saw penalties raining down in the pile-up situation, even when players were being accidentally knocked over, which created large differences of opinion between players and referees. It was seen as a crazy time to be so severe and strict on such an issue, and it was definitely against the interests of the northern hemisphere players. Fortunately, the senior referees took a more tolerant and moderate view in the later stages, and we had some great games, but at one point there was so much aggravation between officialdom and the forwards that a number of games were almost ruined. However, it all came out in the wash and we saw memorable moments of high drama, pathos and triumph, and some spectacular rugby.

Without question, the player of the tournament was David Campese, who produced moments of such derring-do, determination and astonishing skill that he left us speechless with admiration. Time and again he took games by the throat and, by the force of his extraordinary personality, drove Australia relentlessly towards not only success, but to a quality of play that was unsurpassed by any other team in the tournament. Campo not only played a good game but talked one as well, for he was Australia's best propagandist and sledger. He, more than anybody, riled both the English media and the England team itself with his proclamation that England were boring, which foolishly caused Geoff Cooke and Will Carling to change their game plan for the final, a folly which, in my opinion, caused England to lose the World Cup.

Scotland enjoyed the very best of fortune when the draw had them playing all their games at Murrayfield. It must have been one of the jammiest draws of all time. This was a tremendous advantage, particularly as we had a very settled side in 1991 after winning the Grand Slam in 1990. We had all the great warriors of that Scottish side, led by our highly respected captain, David Sole. There was the formidable back row of John Jeffrey, Finlay Calder and Derek White, with the impressive Gary Armstrong and Craig Chalmers at half back. My brother Scott and Sean Lineen were a powerful centre pairing and, with Tony Stanger and Iwan Tukalo on the wings, it was a very useful back division. The core of the team had been together for three or four years, so we had the experience and, in my opinion, we did ourselves justice in the 1991 World Cup. Both Scotland and England had progressed after 1987, but England had learned even more than we had and, reorganising cleverly under the management of Geoff Cooke and the coaching of Roger Uttley, they suddenly found players who were prepared to be more dedicated; men like Paul Ackford, Wade Dooley, Brian Moore, Dean Richards, Peter Winterbottom and Mike Teague. They became the core of the England pack which dominated British Rugby for a number of years in the early Nineties, and they were also the nucleus of the Lions pack in 1989.

It is interesting to note that, similarly, when the Welsh team toured New Zealand in 1969 and were well beaten, the same Welshmen became the hard core of the successful Lions in New Zealand in 1971. Like those Welshmen, the English forwards were to learn the same lessons, which was a marvellous achievement, for if people can learn to put defeat to good use and come back within a year or so and do extremely well, then you have to admire them for their sense of purpose and their willpower.

There has always been underlying talent in four Home Unions rugby. It was a question of how to harness and improve it, and to build a sense of determination which said, 'We are really going to work hard together and put it right.' I am a great believer that the team is only as strong as its weakest member. If you have any feeble members, then you simply are not going to have a strong side. In 1987 in New Zealand and in 1991 at Twickenham there were no weak members among the New Zealand and Australian teams; they were all very, very good players.

We in the Scottish Squad had worked hard and we were in better shape for this World Cup than we were for the first. I repeat, we could not have had a better draw than to play all our games at Murrayfield and, in addition, we were in a relatively easy pool with Ireland, Japan, and Zimbabwe.

We opened with Japan and took 47 points off them, conceding nine, so it was a super win. The Japanese came at us pretty hard in the first 20 minutes, but then we showed ruthlessness and played some extremely hard rugby, with which the diminutive Japanese simply could not compete. It is remarkable how faithful the Japanese are to Rugby Union football, considering they have experienced so many heavy defeats at the hands of the Caucasian countries. They are terrific rugby players but they suffer terribly from the Bonsai miniature tree syndrome.

We went on to play Zimbabwe and, as we knew we were in for another comparatively easy ride, we rested a number of our senior players but still managed to win comfortably by 51–12. Again we wanted to be ruthless and to rub noses in the score. There was a hardness and a desire in every member of the squad to go out and perform at a level that we had not achieved before. One of the secrets of the World Cup, especially in the pool matches, is consistency and therefore we were determined not to mess about but to play every team we met with the same degree of determination and intensity, no matter how strong, or how weak, they were.

Zimbabwe, who had qualified by beating Ivory Coast,

Morocco and Tunisia in the African Zone, were very disappointing. They conceded 50 points in all three pool matches and lost to Japan by 52–8, which was a bigger defeat than the 51–12 against Scotland. This was Japan's first ever victory at the World Cup Finals and their biggest win in a major International. Up to that point, their score of nine tries was a record in the 1991 World Cup.

Our third pool match was against Ireland, who knew that if they came to Murrayfield and lost then, as runners-up in the pool, they would play their quarter final match at home in Lansdowne Road. Likewise, we Scots knew that if we won, we would play our quarter final match at Murrayfield. We were aware that only some seven months previously, when the two teams had met at Murrayfield, we had scraped home by only 28–25 and many critics had said that we were lucky. However, the Irish had brought some 15,000 supporters with them, and if anyone thought that they were only going to show up and then lose meekly so that they would get the qualifying tie at Lansdowne Road, then they merely had to observe the exchanges during the first half-hour of what was a grim and intense battle.

This fierce match to decide the pool winners was a terrific game of rugby which we won 24–15, and Ralph Keyes became the first player to pass 50 points in the 1991 World Cup, while that great Irish Warrior and lock forward, Donal Lenihan, became the seventh Irishman to reach 50 caps. I thought the game was dramatically influenced when a high ball went up and a Finlay Calder follow-up knocked Staples into oblivion. The very next time we put the ball in the air it bounced off Staples' shoulder into the arms of Graham Shiel, who scored after coming on as a replacement. Ultimately we won and the Scottish crowd, who had given us colossal support, were delighted that we were undefeated in all our pool matches. We were into the quarter final the following week and, once again, playing on our own patch.

That win pitched us against the dreaded Western Samoans, who had made such a name for themselves by knocking Wales about physically and dumping them out of the tournament. They had also succeeded in roughing up Australia who, strangely, had never before played Western Samoa. Only a team with the resolution of the ultimate winners of the competition could have withstood the onslaught. In driving rain, Australia won in the end by nine points to three, in a totally absorbing match which showed that these islanders from the very heart of Polynesia, a series of small islands north-east of Fiji with a total population of only about 170,000, were no South Sea Bubble but extremely dangerous opponents.

It was a remarkable experience, because we were not quite sure what to expect. I knew many of the Western Samoan side and realised that some of them had played for New Zealand in the Hong Kong Sevens and that a number of them were playing Provincial rugby in New Zealand. In fact, the Western Samoan Rugby Union had trawled through the New Zealand Provinces and one felt that they had come up with what was almost a New Zealand 'A' team, a sort of second-best All Blacks side. Such is the potent effect of the Pacific Islands, particularly Samoa, in New Zealand Rugby that nowadays they are almost half of the All Blacks team, where their influence should never be underestimated.

We knew that the Samoans had acquired the reputation of being big hitters and we took that to heart. Scotland, therefore, wanted to acquire our own reputation for vigour and we decided that we would do the knocking about. I remember on the morning of the match waking up at our headquarters at the Dalmahoy Golf and Country Club and hearing Jim Telfer say, 'Listen, what we are going to do is this. When we are playing into this wind [and it was a very strong wind which was blowing straight down the field], you, Gavin, are going to be standing off the rucks and mauls, and you are going to go crashing in and we will play the game within the restricted area around the forwards, and try to smash our way through the Western Samoan underbelly.' It worked like a charm.

In fact, from the very first kick off, we got the ball back from a ruck and I took a short ball to crash through about three or four would-be Samoan tacklers, which really set the scene for the whole of the rest of the first-half performance. It worked, and that was probably one of the most calculated episodes that I have ever been involved in with the Scottish team; the end result was that we had simply smashed Western Samoa physically to win 28–6. It only shows what you can do when you set your mind to it but I do not think that many sides could have beaten Samoa by as many points as we did that day, for we were implacably determined and remorseless in our approach. We took every scoring opportunity that came our way and the Samoans were humbled by the experience.

I believe that was one of the best victories by Scotland that I have been part of. A majority of those Samoans play rugby of a higher standard, week in and week out, than the Scottish players can ever hope to – and yet, somehow, the collective team spirit, the organisational skills and the tactics of the Scottish team that were employed in those early exchanges were such that we were able to win comfortably. The Samoans were extremely popular visitors and they thoroughly deserved their lap of honour around Murray- field, as it was an extraordinary achievement for such a small nation to get to the quarter finals. They are an example to every- body in world rugby of what can be achieved by a very small nation indeed.

It was rather strange being on tour in our own country, so to speak, but we certainly were not complaining as we felt that we had a more than even chance of winning any match at Murrayfield, and it almost worked out like that, apart from that fateful semi-final. We based ourselves at two hotels, staying up at St Andrews at the Old Course Hotel, which is a beautiful hostelry overlooking the 17th, or the famous road hole. We used to go up there on a Sunday afternoon, and then we would come back down to Dalmahoy and stay Wednesday, Thursday, Friday and Saturday.

After beating Samoa we had another week to prepare for the semi-final clash against England, so we started off by unwinding and relaxing at St Andrews, before returning to Dalmahoy and composing ourselves for what we had to do on the Saturday. The people at Dalmahoy and the whole nation really got behind us. We were on the news every night and in the papers every day.

It was a new experience for the Scottish rugby players to enjoy such a high profile and I believe that it was a dawning of a new era of Scottish Rugby. The Grand Slam in 1990 had been the start of it but there had not been the same continuity of wide- spread media exposure received by the players as in the World Cup, which saw sustained attention over a period of four or five weeks. It was a tremendous atmosphere in which to be involved, with a great group of players and two of the finest coaches in the world, Ian McGeechan and Jim Telfer. It was an intensely exciting and fulfilling period of my life, and it was a marvellous experience and a privilege to be part of it.

The semi-final of the World Cup could have been written by a thriller writer, because it was against the 'Auld Enemy', the English, a re-run of the 1990 Grand Slam match at Murrayfield 18 months before. Tickets were as scarce as a 50-year-old bottle of whisky – the demand was unprecedented. The capacity of Murray- field had been reduced to a mere 54,000 due to the regulations of the Safety of Sportsgrounds Act. The day was dull but dry and there were visitors from all over the world, including our most faithful patron, Her Royal Highness the Princess Royal, with her children Peter and Zara, which made the singing of our rugby anthem, *Flower of Scotland*, and the National Anthem, a poignant and a stirring moment.

I have never played in a match, either before or since, with as much pressure, hype and passion as that which surrounded this game. I felt that we should do something similar to the slow walk on to the field in 1990 to try and undermine the English and make them understand that here we were again, a team that intended to win the World Cup. We all recognised that it would be one of the hardest games of rugby of our lives but after our performance against Western Samoa the week before, we possessed a great deal of confidence.

It was an unusual feature of the match that neither team was led on to the field by their captain, as Rory Underwood led out England in recognition of being the first Englishman to win 50 caps, while we were led out by that mighty man, John Jeffrey, Scotland's most capped flanker of all time, with 39 caps. The White Shark was playing his last International at Murrayfield, where he had graced the game for so long with his voracious marauding and where he had built up a tremendous understanding with Finlay Calder and Derek White to form one of Scotland's finest back row trios of all time. John also possessed the Scottish record of tries in Internationals by a forward until Derek caught up with him the following season.

Our preparations had gone well and I was confident with my goal kicking. We always used to go into the team-room at Dalmahoy prior to leaving for the ground. We were changed ready for the game and Ian McGeechan gave us his final words of wisdom. On this particular day no one quite knew what to expect from him, but he merely put on a video tape showing all the best moments of Scotland playing England and we left the supercharged atmosphere of that team-room knowing that we were ready and confident. When we arrived at Murrayfield there were already thousands of people milling around and you could just sense the tingling expectancy and excitement in the atmosphere.

Looking back, I realise it was the hardest game of rugby I had ever played in, for I got an absolute doing from the England forwards. In the first minute Rob Andrew hoisted the ball, I caught it and was tackled, and the whole of the England pack simply ran over me and gave me a terrific shoeing. That was the way both teams knew the game was going to be played, so intense, so physical, so hard, with no quarter asked or given and no prisoners taken because so much was at stake. It did not, however, go beyond the limits of that thin line of demarcation which divides vigour from downright dirty play. In no way was it a vicious game, just a hard, hard game of rugby.

We knew that we were going to have great difficulty in the scrummage and the line-out, and laid our plans accordingly. Against England's powerhouse pack, we decided to get the ball out of the scrum as quickly as possible and to give England as few line-outs as possible by not kicking to touch, and so we punted only into the space behind the English forwards.

The match was no classic for the spectators, as both teams stuck grimly to tactical plans, which entailed a great deal of kicking, both by us and by Rob Andrew, who is one of the best kickers of the ball in world rugby. It was, therefore, not a pretty sight. Scotland achieved a 6–0 lead after I kicked two penalty goals. Jonathan Webb, who only managed to kick two out of six attempts at penalties, now kicked a goal to make it 6–3 at half-time. Seventeen minutes into the second half, he kicked another and we were locked at six-all.

Scotsmen will probably always remember that I then missed the simplest of penalties in front of the posts, with only 18 minutes to go, which would have taken us into a 9–6 lead. Englishmen will remember the game for Rob Andrew's drop goal which clinched the match with five minutes to go, to equal the world record for drop goals along with Naas Botha, Hugo Porta and Lescarboura in major Internationals.

Talk about outrageous fortune, but that miss was the most crucial of my life. There was almost 20 minutes to go when we had the opportunity of going ahead again with that penalty. I remember coming into the back line in a move just before taking that kick and getting absolutely smoked by Mickey Skinner, who, in his manner, flattened me in a tackle typical of the intensity of the battle. For a while I was dazed. I do not want to make excuses, but perhaps I did not really have time to recover and compose myself. Nevertheless that miss was down to me, and although it will not haunt me for the rest of my life, it was still desperate to see it slip by. However, it is one of those things, for when you are so close to the posts and you get your kick just slightly off target, there is no time for it to draw back. That kick was six inches to the right of the post and, to my undying horror, it stayed there. I felt awful. I knew that it was the very worst moment of my rugby life.

I remember going into the dressing-room at the end of the game, and, when I took off my jersey, my back was like the road map of Britain, with all the scrapes and stud marks. It just showed how physical the game had been. I sat on one side of the changing-room for an hour without moving. I was very, very sore, very, very disappointed, and mentally and physically exhausted. I resigned myself there and then to the fact that, although people may blame me for the defeat, I knew I could not have played any better as an individual. As I sat there, I said to myself that I would be back at work the following week, that I was not mentally or physically scarred for life and that it was only a game. Thus, I put things into proper perspective by realising that I could not have tried any harder, and indeed neither could the Scottish team. We had given it our best shot and our supporters had been magnificent.

I had to put up with all the usual questions from the Press, and then went and had a night out in Edinburgh. Sometimes, coming out of a defeat, you have a time that summarises all the great things about rugby, for you then take comfort from your team-mates and your friends. That night, it was just the Scottish team together, after we had a joint dinner with the English side. Not unnaturally, they had their minds elsewhere and they sort of disappeared, knowing that they had earned an inalienable right to a place in the final after soldiering so successfully and bravely at Parc des Princes and Murrayfield.

The next day we travelled down to Cardiff for the third and fourth place play-off match. We watched the other semi-final between Australia and New Zealand live on the Sunday afternoon, and it was probably the most powerful match of the whole tournament. It was even perceived by some, at the time, as being the true final. It was incredibly competitive, entirely in the style of southern hemisphere Test matches and it was graced by the genius of two individuals. One was David Campese, who throughout the tournament seemed to commit himself entirely to the winning of it. He not only scored a dazzling opening try, but, with Michael Lynagh, conjured up the try of the tournament for Tim Horan. The other, the Australian captain Nick Farr-Jones, remarkably recovered from a serious knee injury sustained against Samoa, was also at his authoritative best. Anyway, Australia comprehensively beat New Zealand and we then knew that we were going to have to play the All Blacks in the play-off – a pretty daunting prospect at any time, but we were now in the mood and ready to play anybody.

On the Sunday night we, the players, felt that we were ready for a few beers in the Cardiff pubs. We were staying in the Angel Hotel and Jim Telfer called us into the tea-room for a talk. Ian McGeechan had gone home for some reason, and Jim told us, 'I think there are a lot of you who feel that the World Cup is over. In two days time, you are going to play the second hardest game that you have ever had to play in your lives and, if any of you think that you are going out for a few beers tonight, then you had better think again.' It just showed the stature of Jim Telfer that, to a man, each of the players respected his decision and, putting the disappointment of the previous day behind us, we stayed in the hotel and vowed that we would go out and play the game of our lives against New Zealand.

We came close to beating them, and the score was 9–6 with only minutes to go, from three penalty goals from Jon Preston and two by myself; and then, with three minutes to go, Walter Little scored a try to clinch the match. Again Scotland had played extremely well. Somehow we had managed to put the defeat by England behind us, but let me say that it was not easy to raise our game again only a matter of four days after the semi-final loss. We had a great party that night; our World Cup was over but we had enjoyed the experience and we were able to hold our heads up very high.

In the play-off match against New Zealand, I missed another kick in front of the posts and I was furious with myself. Then I remember New Zealand taking a long drop out which I gathered and, charging down the touchline, I saw Richard Loe, the famed and fearsome New Zealand prop, in front of me. Normally I would have kicked the ball ahead and chased after it, but I was so inflamed that I basically did the old Maori side-step and ran right over the top of him. I heard the deep whoosh of expelling breath as he was flattened. Because it took place right in front of the cameras, television kept showing this fearsome New Zealand prop getting wiped out by a humble Scottish full back. I remember Richard Loe coming up to me after the game and saying, 'Christ, mate, you really embarrassed me today. Best that I do not mention your missed kicks in front of the posts and that you do not mention my attempted tackle.' We had a good laugh and we shared a few beers that night, which is one of the nice things about rugby. But I enjoyed that moment; I think it summed up my frustration and disappointment over those fateful four days.

On the Thursday before the final, the Scottish Rugby Union put us up in a pleasant hotel and flew the girls down for the final at Twickenham. You have to remember that we were on tour while we were in Scotland, which was pretty monastic, so we had not seen much of our wives and girlfriends. It was lovely, therefore, to have a couple of days with them in London prior to the final.

When we got off the coach which took us to Twickenham for the game, there was a salesman selling Australian scarves and hats so, probably still being a bit miffed by our defeat at the hands of the 'Auld Enemy', we all rushed over and bought Australian scarves. That obviously upset many English supporters in the West car park and they could not believe that the Scottish team were going to support Australia. I also know, for a fact, for the first time in their lives, the Australians were even being supported by the New Zealanders, which was quite remarkable, as the rivalry between Australia and New Zealand is as great as between England and Scotland. At any rate I certainly felt that it was natural enough for the Scots to support the opposition to the team we had lost to in the semi-final. There was no malice in it, it was just a bit of a laugh, but many of the England team took our behaviour rather badly.

From the moment they kicked off and England, the first time they won the ball, swung it out to their backs, I knew that they were going to lose. I simply could not believe that England, at the behest of the media, would change their tactics for the final, but they did. All week the Aussies, led by their sledger-in-chief, David Campese, were declaring that England were boring and too restricted in their play to win the tournament. They should have known better, for as soon as the Australians said something like that, it implied that they were worried about England playing their power game. I therefore believe that it was a matter of England losing the World Cup rather than Australia winning it. Nevertheless Australia were by far the most attractive side of the World Cup. The vastly experienced Bob Dwyer and Bob Templeton had manipulated the Press, and England were outdone and out-smarted by the Australian con artists. If they had stuck to their original game, I have no doubt that England would have won the World Cup.

CHAPTER VII

A Famous Pride

DURING THE 1988/89 SEASON leading up to the Lions Tour, I was struggling with a bad groin injury and I missed the whole of the Five Nations tournament that year. I did the damage at the beginning of December and thought it was not too serious, so I went off on a long planned skiing trip to Vail in Colorado, as I fancied a bit of relaxation and recuperation. However, I came back to London, where I was living at the time, realising that my injury was more serious than I had first thought, and eventually I went to a specialist for advice and treatment.

Some people said at the time that I was a fool to go skiing because there was no easier way of damaging my groin, but it was not like that at all. I am sure it did not help, but the long and the short of it was that I got the injury diagnosed and it was a long process to get back to full fitness. For two months I did nothing very much, but then I went down to the athletic track at Tooting Bec and met Mike Mein, who brought me back to full fitness. He later became the fitness coach at Rosslyn Park and then went on to Harlequins. Some of us would go down to the track – Peter Winterbottom, Richard Moon, Mark Thomas, Nick Chesworth and I were always there, and Mickey Skinner occasionally. A few of us used to train fairly regularly and none more so than myself, that year, because I was unable to play and needed to build up my fitness, but I had to be careful and could only run in straight lines in order to avoid straining my groin.

Peter Dods was playing well for Scotland, Jonathan Webb

was showing a lot of attacking flair for England, while Paul Thorburn was captain of Wales at the time, so I thought to myself, I am going to be struggling to get on this Lions Tour as I am not going to be playing an awful lot of rugby between now and the selection of the tour party, and certainly not in the Five Nations. All I could do was to get myself really fit and take it from there. However, I only played my first game in April, but by then I had already been named in the Lions party, together with Peter Dods, who had an extremely fine Five Nations Championship for Scotland after missing three years and having to sit on the bench while I was playing full back in the Scottish side. I am sure Paul Thorburn and Jonathan Webb were bitterly disappointed at missing out. However, Peter had played so well that year and his goal kicking was such that he deserved his selection.

I remember coming back and playing my first game for London Scottish against Leicester at Richmond, not an easy game in which to return, but to my intense relief I got through it. We then had a Lions Squad weekend, in which we had a lot of fitness testing, including the dreaded BEEP test, for which I got the highest rating I ever achieved, about 15 – I have gone downhill ever since. It is a bloody hard test, involving a 20-metre progressive shuttle run to exhaustion and produces an indirect measurement of aerobic power, but it is probably better that you do not know too much about it.

One of the best things about the 1989 Lions, from my point of view, was that Finlay Calder had been chosen as captain, because I knew he was a disciplinarian and how dedicated he would be. He would certainly have the players' respect. Welshman Clive Rowlands was manager, another Scot, Ian McGeechan, was coach, and Roger Uttley, an Englishman, was the assistant coach. There was a strong, powerful and experienced group of English forwards, with Wade Dooley, Paul Ackford, Mike Teague, Brian Moore and Dean Richards among the large English contingent, and there was a pretty strong representation from Scotland after an encouraging Five Nations Championship. There were nine Scots in the party, including Gary Armstrong and Craig Chalmers, who were very young, which was to give a tremendous boost to the future of Scottish Rugby. Astonishingly, only Robert Norster and Donal Lenihan had been on a Lions Tour before and, therefore, most of us were going into the unknown. However both coaches, Ian McGeechan and Roger Uttley, had been Lions in the Seventies and knew what it was all about.

It was all very exciting, for we did not know how good Australia were going to be. It turned out that it was one of the hardest tours I have ever been on. We knew that Australia had achieved the Grand Slam in the British Isles in 1984 and that, in 1988 when they again came over, England had beaten them convincingly by 28–19 but, to our chagrin, they had easily beaten Scotland by 32–13. In the summer of 1988 England lost both Tests in Australia fairly substantially, so we had a shrewd feeling that life with the Lions in Australia was not going to be easy.

Looking back, it was a lovely country to visit on a tour and it was hugely enjoyable, largely because the man in the street in Australia knows little about Rugby Union. You can walk around town without being recognised, nobody knows who you are, so it is a great deal more relaxed, off the field, than touring New Zealand or South Africa.

Having said that, the rugby establishment in Australia seemed to know more about the game than most rugby administrators in the British Isles, and they have become a mainstream country in terms of innovation, while their coaches are far more go-ahead, imaginative, inventive and progressive than their counterparts in the UK. But then they have to be, because of the huge competition from Australian Rules and Rugby League, which makes Rugby Union the Cinderella game. They must find new ideas in order to encourage their players to stay with Rugby Union and to attract public support in the face of the fierce competition from these rival codes. For that reason they had a special dispensation of not being allowed to kick the ball directly into touch between the two 25s. It was amazing that it took the rest of us and the lawmakers all those years to introduce it into the current laws of the game.

I remember, too, that back in the Seventies they introduced a unique penalty move into the game, called 'Up Your Jumper'. This entailed a huddle after a penalty was awarded, during which somebody stuck the ball inside his jersey after the tap, and they all exploded like a star shell to various parts of the field as the opposition desperately tried to identify the ball carrier. Inevitably, however, it was stamped on by the International Board as not being in the spirit of the game. The spectators who saw it being employed thought it was an absolute scream and, for a season or two, they had a lot of success and fun with this unusual, but typically Aussie, move.

If Australia played only Rugby Union, then they would be

absolutely dynamic and both New Zealand and South Africa could lose their world dominance. It is fortunate for the rest of the rugby world that they have other distractions. It is strange that, although young Australians can play on a world stage in the Rugby Union game, they still cling tenaciously and faithfully to the more incestuous Australian Rules, which is only played in Australia and is a close relation to the Irish Gaelic football, from which it was derived. Rugby League is also a major game, whereas it is virtually played in only two counties of England, a little in France and South Africa, where it is failing, and in New Zealand, where it is growing due to the influence of Australian television, and also in Papua New Guinea, where it is not all that strong. It seems incomprehensible, but perhaps it has something to do with the sheer bloody-mindedness and independent streak which is so characteristic of the Aussie mentality.

In the past, League has attracted many very good Australian Union players into the professional game, but I believe that is changing now that Union is becoming more organised and more professional. Recently, the Australian Rugby Union arranged a huge sponsored dinner and brochure for the players' fund for the 1993 season. The target was half a million dollars.

As I have said, this was a really hard tour, not by virtue of the Provincial games, which, apart from New South Wales and Queensland, are nothing like the continual challenge you meet in New Zealand, but because the three Tests were so abrasively and bitterly fought and we faced some fierce whingeing from the Australian Press. However, that only told us that we had them on the run and served to increase our motivation to win the series, particularly after we had lost the first Test. The whole series, though, finally established Australia as a realistic and genuine venue for a Lions Tour. Much of this was due to the success of the Wallabies in the British Isles in 1984, which awakened Australian awareness of Rugby Union Football in their country in a way that never before had been achieved.

Finlay Calder, our captain, did a terrific job in creating a will to win in the touring party. A hard-headed man, he spared no one, himself included, in his determination to win the series, and therefore we acquired a great deal of self-belief. He was fortunate that he had a hard core of English forwards who had been in Australia the year before and not only knew the form, but wanted to get in a bit of revenge. In Dean Richards, Mike Teague, Paul Ackford and Brian Moore, he had some really battle-hardened troops and

The Brothers Hastings with Geech, North Sydney Oval, Australia, 1989

White water rafting, North Queensland, 1989. Chilcott and Hastings with Ackford and Dooley behind and Rob Andrew with Dr Ben Gilfeather bringing up the rear

In Sydney with the Lions in 1989

Three Scottish captains enjoying the dirt-tracker life in Cairns in 1989

On the charge against the ANZAC XV with Scott and John Devereux in close support (photograph: Kenji Ito)

A hat-trick of tries: (top) for Scotland against France at Murrayfield, 1988; (bottom left) for the Lions against Australia, Ballymore, 1989, and congratulations from Ieuan Evans (photograph: Bob Thomas); (bottom right) on the way to scoring against Japan in the World Cup, Murrayfield, 1991

Grand Slam 1990: Slains coming close to charging down my clearance kick (photograph: Daily Record*)*

Grand Slam 1990: 'My ball, Jeremy' (photograph: Daily Record*)*

Grand Slam 1990: The Shark closing in on Richard Hill with Derek White waiting for left-overs (photograph: Daily Record*)*

Grand Slam 1990: 'We've done it!' with John Jeffrey at No Side (photograph: Daily Record*)*

Grand Slam 1990: Let the celebrations begin! (photograph: Daily Record*)*

Boys' night out, Christmas 1991: Gavin Hastings, David Sole, David Milne, Sean Lineen, Ivan Tukalo, Scott Hastings (photograph: Daily Record*)*

Scott, Ivan Tukalo and I prepare for battle (photograph: Daily Record*)*

Sean trying to remember the second verse of 'Flower of Scotland', Murrayfield, 1991 (photograph: Daily Record*)*

Richards and Teague, in particular, were the players of the tour.

We landed in Perth to play against what was virtually an ex-pat New Zealand XV and, in spite of the usual scaremongering, we won handsomely by 44–0. It was encouraging to get off to such a good start, but I always remember how hard we trained in the first week of the tour, for it is essential to let everybody know that this is why you are there. Exacting tours always demand a price and in Perth we lost the Irish outside half Paul Dean, which meant that Rob Andrew was flown out as a replacement. In the end, this proved extremely fortuitous because, although we had the very talented fly half Craig Chalmers at hand, he simply was not ready for Test match rugby with the Lions. In the event, Rob Andrew was quick to take his opportunity and make a name for himself.

We moved on to Melbourne and played a so-called Australian 'B' team on a filthy wet night at Olympic Park. Our opponents included about nine Australian Internationals, and the team selected to play them had to go really hard to win 23–18. With only three weeks from the first game to the first Test, every game was important and the first big watershed came in Brisbane against Queensland, who had already beaten New South Wales by over 30 points. The Lions were indebted to the front row of David Sole, Brian Moore and David Young for breaking the Queensland scrummage. Robert Jones scored the only try of the game, Craig Chalmers dropped two goals and I kicked three penalties. The disappointing aspect of the game was that although our pack had a storming game, our backs appeared less than dangerous. This was to prove a disappointing feature of the tour, at the end of which Ian McGeechan expressed regret that he had had insufficient time to develop the back play. There was also the factor that the Australians, in recent years, have developed a remarkable midfield swarm defence, against which everybody is finding it difficult to score.

We then had a pleasant jaunt up to Cairns, near the Barrier Reef, to play Queensland 'B' for a comfortable victory. It also afforded us with one of those valuable days away from rugby, when we visited the Barrier Reef and many of the team took the opportunity to go scuba diving or snorkelling, before going to Sydney for another serious game against New South Wales. By their standards it had been a very poor, wet winter in Australia, so they had a problem finding a ground dry enough in the whole of Sydney. They eventually found one on the north side, called the North Sydney Oval, where the North Sydney Bears, the Rugby

League side, played, and which was also a cricket ground. It was a superb stadium and on a magnificent day they filled it with about 30,000 spectators.

We were winning the game quite comfortably until midway through the second half, when suddenly their legendary winger David Campese got involved, and we saw a comfortable lead of 20 points to twelve whittled away. We were actually losing 21–20 after Marty Roebuck kicked five penalties and converted his own try. Fortunately we won the game when Craig Chalmers dropped a timely goal deep into injury time. Nevertheless we had posted due warning that we were a team to be reckoned with. We had an easy match against New South Wales 'B' in midweek, up country at Dubbo, and flew back to Sydney to confidently face the Aussies in the first Test.

There was a full house at the new and imposing Sydney Football Stadium, and it was the first time that they had sold out. Talk about putting in a below par performance! We were humiliated and hammered by 30–12. It was a great shock to our system. I can recall going back to the changing-room after the game, where Clive Rowlands got everybody together, and in his intense Welsh voice said, 'Right, boys, we have suffered a huge defeat and now there is only one way to go.' We all resolved there and then to win the two remaining Test matches and turn the tour around. All the players, the subs and the rest of the squad agreed and vowed, 'Yes, we can do it.' It was a tremendous example of the Lions' team spirit on the other side of the world. After suffering a great indignity, we pledged that we would not be beaten again and we kept our word by going through the rest of the tour undefeated. We won the remaining two Tests and the ANZAC game, which was supposed to be an amalgam of the best Wallaby and All Black players, though the New Zealanders let Australia down by not turning up in any force. You could put it all down to the resolve we showed in that changing-room, but it must also be remembered that we played the first Test without a number of key players who were injured, notably Mike Teague, Paul Ackford, Scott Hastings and Jeremy Guscott.

Before leaving for Brisbane for the second Test, we went to Canberra to play the Australian Capital Territory, ACT in short. This became another test of resolve, for at half-time the Lions were losing 21–11 after playing the worst 40 minutes of the whole tour. The Lions' forwards then went to town and virtually battered their opponents, to defeat them by 41–25. The Lions were heavily criticised by the local Press for the hardness of their forward play, for never using their backs and for the fact that their last three scores were three penalty goals by Peter Dods.

The Test team was announced on the Friday, with five changes from the previous Saturday, Wade Dooley and Mike Teague taking over from Bob Norster and Derek White. The whole midfield trio was changed, and Craig Chalmers, Mike Hall and Brendan Mullin were replaced by Rob Andrew, Scott Hastings and Jerry Guscott.

We thought that we had been roughed up a bit in the first Test in the forwards and we were determined to sort things out – and that we did. There was no more trouble on the tour after that, for we showed Australia in that second Test at Ballymore who was boss, in what became a bitter and ferocious Test match. Although the Lions trailed by 12–9 until the last five minutes, due to some fine goal kicking from Michael Lynagh, it was the Welsh scrum half, Robert Jones, who turned the tide with some marvellous kicking into the box, at which he is a master; and in the final dramatic minutes I scored what turned out to be the winning try, followed by another from Jerry Guscott, to seal the Lions victory 19–12.

It had been an extremely fierce and abrasive Test match which again had the Australian Press whingeing and sledging the Lions and saying that they had behaved like hooligans. All this achieved was to tell us that Australians were now really worried, because we had redressed the balance after our first Test defeat and we were firm favourites to win the third and deciding Test.

I remember that I got concussed near to half-time and played the whole of the second period in a daze. I scored the try which put us into the lead, which was followed by another by Jeremy Guscott. When, at full-time, I walked off the pitch to be asked by the reporters to talk them through the try, I could not remember scoring it, though I had the wit to say, 'I will talk to you later about that.' I then went back to the hotel and watched it on television so that I could comment, for, seriously, I could not remember scoring it. It was, in fact, a typical pass from my brother Scott, one of his normal ones which bounced about 40 times along the ground before it came up into my arms.

After a welcome short break on the Gold Coast at Surfers Paradise, we were back to Sydney for the final showdown, again at the Sydney Football Stadium. It was a match to stretch the nerves, for we scraped home 19–18, after some of the hardest pressure rugby that most of us had played up to that time. It was, perhaps, to be superseded by the World Cup semi-finals and the British Lions Tests in New Zealand, but at that time, because of the expectation that we were going to win, we employed a huge amount of passion and nervous energy, as it was a desperately close game. Happily for me, I kicked extremely well and put over five penalty goals, which was the best I had kicked all tour.

The only other Lions score was a try by Ieuan Evans, which was the most talked about of the series. Having haunted David Campese throughout the series, he now managed to force him into a dreadful indiscretion, doing something stupid on his own line when he threw a wretched pass to his full back Greg Martin. They say that virtue is its own reward and Ieuan, who had consistently pressured Campo, hit the jackpot when he grasped the loose ball for what, at the time, was a decisive try. For his part, Campese received the most terrible calumny from the Australian Press, who rounded on him for losing a crucial Test match, forgetting all the ones that he had helped Australia to win with his great genius. Mark Ella produced the most witty one-liner when he said on the radio, 'One day "wonderman", next day "blunderman".' Ieuan Evans is the consummate competitor and he showed on the Lions Tours of 1989 and 1993 what a marvellous player he is.

It is interesting to note that from the third Test in 1989 in Australia to the third Test in New Zealand in 1993, there was considerable continuity and consistency from the players involved. In the forwards, Brian Moore and Dean Richards played in both those Tests and, in the backs, so did Rob Andrew, Rory Underwood, Ieuan Evans, Jeremy Guscott and I. We had become the first Lions to win a Test series since the 1974 team in South Africa. We had also become the first Lions to win a series after losing the first Test, but so close was it that at the end I only had a feeling of great relief rather than one of euphoria.

Penultimately, we had to play New South Wales Country team, which we hammered by 72–13, and ultimately the ANZACs, a sort of Antipodean Barbarians, which in the end included only three New Zealanders. It was far from an easy game and we scraped home by 19–15 to end my first Lions Tour, which had given us all so much pleasure, together with a great sense of achievement and fulfilment.

I kept a personal diary of every day of the tour and, in order to give you some impression of life with the Lions, here are some of my entries during the period of the Test matches.

TUESDAY 27 JUNE:

Again a beautiful morning and, as it was a match day, the non-selected players trained for an hour prior to a team meeting. We left for the ground, already changed into our kit, only half an hour before kick off, owing to a lack of changing facilities at the ground. The pitch itself was excellent and there was a decent crowd of about 5,000 people. As usual, we were under pressure for the first quarter but scored a lucky try, which gave us more momentum. Too often, however, we were penalised for ill-discipline and after establishing a 25–6 lead we let them back in at 25–19, before scoring three very good tries. After the game it was straight back to the motel for a shower and change prior to a boring function and then a meal, which was only slightly better. We had a decent sing-song for a couple of hours, until bed.

WEDNESDAY 28 JUNE:

Dai Young, who was duty boy, woke me at about 7.45 a.m. Made a couple of phone calls. After breakfast the Test team was announced prior to training, with, in my opinion, two shock selections, Mike Hall at centre and Derek White at blind side. It was a good productive session in glorious weather.

After a shower we packed and went to a barbie at some guy's house before catching our mid-afternoon flight to Sydney. After having had a good feed the boys were in fine fettle on the flight, singing their way to Sydney, and it was back to the Camperdown Travel Lodge, which was not one of our favourite hotels. We had dinner and a team meeting before an early night.

THURSDAY 29 JUNE:

I woke with my back in a complete spasm and very painful, so I missed the intensive training session out at Randwick. Again it was a bright morning and the team trained hard in preparation for the Test. After lunch, I stayed in all afternoon and had treatment from Smurf (our Physio, Kevin Murphy), before a further team meeting at 5.30 p.m. We concentrated on the Australia v New Zealand Test match of the previous year, which I thought was pretty hopeless. Scott and I went to a friend's for a meal with Mum and Dad. It was good to get out of the hotel and we had a good laugh, and excellent food and drink. Went back to the folks' hotel in north Sydney before catching a taxi home at about 11 p.m. I was full of the cold – a great preparation for a Test!

FRIDAY 30 JUNE:
Trained at the Sydney Football Stadium and I managed to at least
jog around in front of the Press, as we were now in pre-match
mode. I went on to the main pitch to practise goal kicking and
received my first feel of this superb stadium, and I imagined what
the atmosphere was going to be like. Kicking went well, so I
returned to the hotel in a fairly confident mood. In the afternoon,
we went down to Darling harbour and bought a few T-shirts.
Another team meeting and watched a video before further treatment with Smurf, and bed about 11 p.m.

SATURDAY 1 JULY:
Got up late for breakfast at about nine and read the papers, which
were reasonably favourable to the Lions. Then caught some fresh
air with Dai Young and Finlay, in the early morning cool before
the team meeting. Ate a light lunch and then relaxed in front of
the TV prior to the meeting in the team-room for an inspirational
talk from Geech, which stressed that this would be one of the most
important days of our lives and that we had the chance of going
down in history. We got on the team coach and concentrated on
the task ahead as we travelled the half hour to the stadium.

There were hundreds of people milling around and we
dropped our kit in the spacious changing-rooms and trekked
down the long tunnel out on to the touch line of the new amphi-
theatre. Randwick were playing Easts in the curtain raiser and
there was already a sizeable crowd. We could see the Australian
players stripped and ready as we made our way back up the
tunnel. We were not to know that we would go back the next time
with lowered heads, after the sickness of defeat and the knowledge that we had really blown it; in fact, humiliated by an Aussie
side who had performed really well and kept us under intense
pressure. The manager Clive Rowlands tried to revive our sagging
spirits by vowing we would come back in the next two Tests and
saying that we must accept defeat with honour, but never forget
what happened that afternoon.

I caught up with my brother Graeme and Jacqui, his wife, as
well as Toddy, his friend, at the after-match function and started
getting a few beers down to drown my sorrows. It was fairly
informal and the Aussies were their usual unsociable selves and
sporting mile-wide grins. Mum and Dad came over and sympa-
thised, and we trooped off to the bus, thankful to be on our own
again. The mood was pretty sombre and we tried to sing, but

quickly gave up. On arrival back at the hotel, we held our second court of the tour. Donal Lenihan, as captain of Donal's Donuts, took over as judge from Finlay, who was summarily dealt with and fined. Griff and Dai Young were charged for never being apart and were required to be joined together for the rest of the evening. Wade was fined for having his sister in tow and Brendan was fined for always being in his room and never allowing his room-mates time for a five-fingered massage. Chris Oti was required to do some break dancing.

After dinner, we were back on the team coach, and off to Darling harbour to the James Craig Bar for more Bundys (rums) and general good times. It was a good night at the end of a frustrating day, but our spirits were back and we knew we could still win the series.

SUNDAY 2 JULY:
Robbo and I awoke to the telephone. It was a friend expressing commiserations and whatnot. Robbo and I went to the Sydney Football Stadium for a game of squash and a swim, and it was good to sweat out the excess alcohol from the previous night. Delayed again at Sydney Airport and it was 7 p.m. before we checked into our hotel in Canberra. After a good dinner, we had a quick quiz and most people went off to bed at around nine, to watch various films on TV and to have an early night.

MONDAY 3 JULY:
Training at 9 a.m. for a couple of hours, during which the boys worked really hard. It was a rush again as we showered back at the hotel before leaving for the local rugby club for lunch. Although it was a pretty laid back affair and the food was great, it was still nagging into our leisure time, and so we only had three hours to ourselves, during which time some of us visited the Australian Institute of Sport, which was pretty interesting. Alas, it was back in number ones for a visit to the High Commissioner and a few G & Ts, which was not as stuffy as some. Dinner back at the hotel and then a video re-run of Saturday's nightmare before bed.

TUESDAY 4 JULY:
We Dirt Trackers went training at 9.30 a.m. and played football for an hour, and then I took a long bath before having some lunch and walking down to the Seiffert Oval with the rest of the DTs. It was a

strange match and we took our time recovering from 18–4 down before winning substantially. Messed around for two hours before arriving at the official dinner for a pretty awful evening, but things improved when we went to the official opening of the Canberra Raiders Nightclub and had a few cheap Bundys before getting back to bed about 1 a.m.

WEDNESDAY 5 JULY:
Woken at 7 a.m., left at 8.15 a.m. after packing and breakfast, and set off for Brisbane via Sydney. Went to our hotel, the Mayfair, for an hour, before leaving for the country for training some 18km from Brisbane, and then an informal barbecue dinner with a bunch of kids, where we sat with youngsters who played the same positions.

THURSDAY 6 JULY:
Trained on another bright morning at the Brisbane Boys College. The Press were there doing their usual sheep imitations and asking the same stupid questions. After a late lunch, I sat out on the rooftop pool and read a book, while the sun was setting. A reception at the British Consul General's home, for Donal's Donuts, was the biggest booze-up of the tour, while the team for Saturday again watched the previous week's Test. Went out for a pasta at Buzzards and enjoyed a further quiet night, in preparation for Saturday's Test.

FRIDAY 7 JULY:
Another brisk work-out at the BBC. The anticipation was there for the following day and we worked hard for success. Back to the hotel and a change, before going off to the Richard Ellis Office at the Riverside Centre. [I worked for Richard Ellis in London at the time.] Went to lunch at an Italian restaurant until 4 p.m. I had seafood soup and veal with a couple of cappuccinos before going to Friday's for a few squashes. Then back to the Crest and went to the pictures with Dean, Scott and Ieuan, to see *Dead Calm*, and went to bed in a good mood and eager for the following day.

SATURDAY 8 JULY:
Woke up early and went down for a large breakfast about 9 a.m. Went for a walk down to the Riverside Centre for fresh air and a change of scene, prior to the team meeting at 11.30 a.m. Just a plate of soup and a sandwich before packing the bags and heading off

to Ballymore about 1.30 p.m. Geech talked to the team before leaving, to psyche us up for the game, and impressed on us not to make the silly mistakes which marred our performance the previous week.

A police escort got us through on time and we walked on to the pitch in front of the main stand to some cheek and jeers from the partisan Aussies. The warm-up in the dressing-room seemed slow and I could not wait to get on to the pitch. There was a good atmosphere as we sprinted out on to the paddock for a quick run round before the anthems.

The first ten minutes saw some serious fighting between respective forwards. It was our intention not to let their forwards take advantage of us in the early exchanges. This had the desired effect and we won the rucks and mauls comprehensively, which was a significant improvement from the previous week.

Going into the last quarter, we were down 12–6 and I had received a bang on my head, right on half-time. On account of this, Rob Andrew took over the goal kicking and banged over a penalty to make it 12–9. Then two tries in the last five minutes from myself and Jerry Guscott saw us home 19–12, and set up a dramatic scene for Sydney the following week.

There was much joy and relief in the changing-room, for we had all taken part in the most crucial match of our careers. Again there was determination that we would not be carried away with our victory and we knew that the job had still to be finished.

After some rest and recreation in the dressing-room, bumped into Mum and Dad in the car park and they were delighted to be sharing our triumph. The post-match function was the usual boring affair and the speeches were short and humourless. It was obvious that those who had played were absolutely knackered after an intense and extremely physical Test match. Back to the Crest Hotel and a few pre-dinner drinks. The meal was slow and relaxed and some of the guys went round to the Criterion for some Guinness, but I returned to bed suffering somewhat from my knock on the head and my lack of alcohol. We were one-to-one with one to go and I wanted to feel really good for the final Test, so I watched Wimbledon on television and contentedly went to sleep about midnight.

SUNDAY 9 JULY:
Got up bright and breezy about 9 a.m. and took a bath before

packing my bags, which were to be down by 10.15 a.m. Breakfast before we departed for the Ramada Hotel at Surfer's. After checking in, a few of us caught the Gold Coast Limo Service out to Surfer's Paradise Golf Club for 15 holes of relaxing golf. I played pretty crappily with Devs and Scott, and then we had a couple of drinks in the club house. Back in time for dinner and I went to bed early and watched TV before getting a good night's sleep.

MONDAY 10 JULY:
We left for Sea World about 10 a.m. on a dull and overcast morning. On arrival we met the general manager, who welcomed us to Sea World and we set off in pursuit of the Corkscrew Ride, hoping to emulate the feat of the little nutter who rode it 43 times consecutively. After various other rides, we watched the Whale and Dolphin show and the Water Ski show which was very exciting. Returning to the Ramada I felt unwell, so after a glass of lemon squash I went to bed, while the guys had a golf tournament out at Surfer's, which was won by Steve Smith of Ballymena with a fine score of 19 points in nine holes. Some of the guys went waterskiing and jet-skiing. Having missed the fun, I watched *First Blood* before going to bed with a bottle of pills.

TUESDAY 11 JULY:
I woke feeling much better, when we went off for training at a large boys' school, TSS. We had a good two-hour training session, before speaking to a group of pupils with Ieuan and Devs. Then we had a quick lunch before driving north of Surfer's to the Driza-Bone factory, where we had a tour round and were each presented with a coat, which was brilliant. We got back about 5 p.m. and had a team meeting, to watch the first half of Saturday's Test before dinner.

WEDNESDAY 12 JULY:
Up at 8.30 a.m., with bags down by 9.15 a.m., and left by 10 a.m. We drove to Coolangata and, for once, flew on time into Sydney without any hassle. After checking into the much improved North Sydney Travel Lodge, and a quick bowl of soup and sandwiches, we went to a local school to train for a couple of hours. It was a dragging session and, although the same side was announced, we did not train as the team, which I thought was a bit of a waste. Arrived back and showered about 5 p.m. and attempted a team meeting, but as the video did not work it was abandoned. Met a

friend and went out to dinner at Sayle's, a small seafood restaurant on the north shore overlooking the Harbour Bridge. It was a good evening and I got back, hopeful of a continued good time for the next few days.

THURSDAY 13 JULY:
Trained at 9.30 a.m. and it was a disjointed session, with four of the team dropping out. Mistakes were made, but we improved on our passing towards the end. I stayed behind with Rob Andrew to do some goal kicking and Roger and Geech remained with us. After a taxi ride home, a quick shower and lunch, I left with a couple of friends for some holes at the Royal Sydney Golf Club. The weather was fine and I played pretty reasonably for the first time on tour, which matched the surroundings. It was a lovely course and a most relaxing couple of hours. Going back to the hotel I grabbed a burger, before changing into number ones for a dinner at the Caltex Building, a small informal gathering which, nevertheless, imposed upon free time.

FRIDAY 14 JULY:
Went back to the North Sydney Oval for training on a bright sunny morning and had a useful workout for an hour or so. I did a bit of punting with Rob Andrew, but gave the goal kicking a miss, as there were no goal posts to kick at. After the customary wait on the bus for the management to finish the Press conference, we set off for the Travel Lodge and a relaxing afternoon.

I went to get my hair cut and stayed chatting afterwards for 20 minutes or more to the three girls in the shop, and then went back for a team meeting. I got to bed about 11.30 p.m., following a relaxing bath and some preparation for the following day.

SATURDAY 15 JULY:
Woke about 8.30 a.m. feeling pretty good, and down for breakfast and the customary read of the morning papers. It was ugly reading, since the Press had decided to brand the Lions as a bunch of thugs and hooligans, and said that there would be a real battle that afternoon and nothing resembling a rugby match. They also stated that the Australian backs were far superior to the Lions and that, if they could win sufficient ball, then the game would go Australia's way.

I, for one, felt aggrieved at the crap that was printed and it was soon obvious that the whole team were of the same opinion, which really fired them up.

The morning dragged before the normal backs' meeting, but eventually we were on the bus to the Sydney Football Stadium, dreaming of the promise we were hoping to realise. Again there was a huge crowd and, in the short walk from the bus to the changing-rooms, many supporters wished us all the best as we walked tall to our destiny.

This time, however, we all changed in one room, as opposed to splitting between the two for the first Test. We knew that a complete team effort was required to achieve our ambition, for which we had worked so hard. The rest of the squad, the replacements and the coaches, and Clive our manager, wished us all the best as they took their places by the touch line. We were on our own, but we all shared similar feelings and our emotions ebbed and flowed as we concentrated for the final five minutes, before being released into the cauldron of the magnificent stadium.

The 40,000-plus spectators were treated to a match full of tension, drama and excitement, a tremendous experience, which I, for one, had never encountered before. The crowd in the last 20 minutes were at fever pitch and, when the final whistle went with Australia trying to attack from their own line, I knew we had not merely beaten the 15 guys on the other side, but a whole nation which cries out for and demands sporting success at the national level.

The Lions were narrow winners on the day, but we had won the series two-one, to hopefully create the kind of respect and sort of immortality achieved by the 1971 and 1974 tours. I felt we had deserved no less, for rugby has changed dramatically since then and the pressures infinitely magnified. It was a supreme effort to come from 0–1 down and, as we trailed around the pitch in a thank you lap to the British people present, we were happy that they were sharing our moment of triumph.

As I came into the tunnel, Graeme, my brother, was there with Jacqui to congratulate the boys. He was so chuffed! The dressing-room was filled with the British photographers, snapping away at the joyous faces and the ensuing magic moments. It was great to grab a seat and look around the room to see how each person reacted to victory. Some were sipping a cold beer, others stripping off and showering, but everyone was beaming and enjoying the feeling of winning.

Nigel Starmer-Smith interviewed a few of us for TV and then it was back to the Travel Lodge to meet family and friends from Cambridge. Changing into our dress blazers, we went down to the tea-room for champagne and a few beers, prior to going to the Hyatt at Kings Cross for dinner. This was a mixed affair and the service was very slow. I sat with Greg Martin and Steve Cutler and their respective wives, and we downed a few Bundys while waiting for the food. The speeches were finished before the main course was completed and then everyone was milling around talking. I met some pals in the bar afterwards, and proceeded to get the Press guys to buy us Bundys until we were kicked out at 3 a.m. A few of the guys were still there, but most had gone off night-clubbing. We caught a taxi back to the Travel Lodge and went to bed pretty satisfied, at about 4 a.m., after a bloody marvellous day.

The reality of a Lions tour is probably far less glamorous than the expectancy before it all happens. It is, however, a tremendous experience for young men. There is an immense amount of hard work and application, and even, at times, moments of boredom. You have to live with new people and if the relationships are going to be happy and successful, there has to be a lot of give and take. Inevitably, after the final Test, although we had another week to go in Australia, with a game at Newcastle and a final denouement against the combined ANZAC XV, our thoughts quickly turned to going home to friends and loved ones, returning to work and all the difficulties of getting back to normality. I, for one, would not have missed the experience for anything, for it was another glorious episode in what for me has been a marvellous life in rugby.

Chapter VIII

The Pinnacle

WITHOUT DOUBT, the pinnacle of my rugby career was to be selected as captain of the British Lions on their 1993 Tour of New Zealand. It was something that gave me a marvellous sense of personal fulfilment, but at the same time I was also aware of the enormous honour that the British Isles selectors had conferred on me, by recognising that I was the best man in British Rugby to lead the Lions. It was, therefore, an extremely unnerving responsibility and a severe challenge.

It was very interesting that, throughout the Five Nations Championship, during which all our thoughts were on selection of the Lions, all of us, in our various countries, were grimly intent on playing well in order to make sure of selection for the tour. In December 1992 I was informed by Duncan Paterson, the chairman of selectors, that they had made me captain of Scotland for the whole season. At that stage I had no thought of being captain of the Lions and, at the time, there was only one person in everyone's mind. Will Carling was the obvious choice, for after all he had achieved two back-to-back Grand Slams, which had only been done once before in England's history, in 1913 and 1914. I acknowledged that Will was the front runner for the job, but nonetheless felt that I had to offer some competition. I had four games in which to do that.

I was asked at the start of the season what my hopes and ambitions were, as far as Scotland was concerned, and I said that I would be very disappointed if we could not go to Twickenham to play for the Triple Crown. This was based on the assumption that we would win our home matches against Ireland and Wales, which is what happened. Suddenly people were talking about this being the battle of the two captains and whichever captain was triumphant on the day would possibly captain the Lions. Well, Twickenham is definitely our bogey ground and we were beaten again, so bang went the Lions' captaincy, as I thought. But the crunch came for Will Carling when England were comprehensively beaten 17–3 by the Irish. They were completely humiliated on the day and that obviously helped my case. I am sure if England had won then, things might have been different and that Will would have been named the Lions' captain.

I remember the team was due to be announced on the Monday following the Dublin match, and on the Sunday I was watching television when suddenly a phone call came from Geoff Cooke. They were just about to go into the selection and he asked me whether, if the captaincy was offered to me, I would accept it, or would I be happier to go as a player? I was surprised at his attitude and certainly left him in no doubt that if I was offered the captaincy I would consider it to be a great honour and be delighted to accept. The phone went again about two hours later. Ian McGeechan had been told to leave the meeting and again ask me whether, if I was offered the captaincy, I would confirm that I would accept it. I thought to myself, 'Geech, why are you making this phone call?' The only supposition I could make was that he had been asked by the selection committee to confirm Geoff Cooke's earlier call.

Later that evening, Geoff Cooke phoned up and said, 'Congratulations, you are the captain of the 1993 British Lions.' I was thrilled. I phoned my parents, and, together with my wife Diane, we cracked open a bottle of champagne. The team was announced the next day and it was all very exciting. At work for the next couple of days, the telephone simply did not stop ringing, asking me for interviews and photographs. We decided that our public relations company at work would prepare a Press release and we held a press conference to kill a few birds with one stone.

Obviously, there was a lot of speculation in the Press as to whether I was the right man for the job but I was very confident in my own abilities to bring the amalgam of players from the four Home Countries together into a single identity. That was very important, but I had the benefit of having been on the previous Lions tour in 1989, and I think I had the even greater benefit of being known to New Zealand and its rugby people. I had been out there in 1987 for the World Cup with Scotland and stayed to play club rugby for Auckland University. I went back with Scotland in 1990 and returned in 1992, this time with a World XV to celebrate the centenary of the New Zealand Rugby Football Union. I think all those factors were extremely important in advancing my claims for the captaincy and I think it was a decision seen as a good one out in New Zealand. I also believe that I had huge support in the British Isles. Will Carling, I believe, had never played in New Zealand up to that point.

I remember the first training weekend was very difficult for everyone and I felt that I did not want to be heavy about anything, deciding to let the players take their time and get to know each other. The coming together of the best players from all the Home Nations is something very special, and I think that people treat it as such and regard it as a great honour. I certainly did. So it was really just a question of allowing everyone to settle and, with 16 Englishmen in the squad, I did not particularly want to start shouting my mouth off, or anything like that. I felt it was important to get everyone together, to create a pleasant harmony within the squad and to build a powerful team spirit because I knew what we were likely to face in New Zealand, where we were going to have to play some extremely tough rugby. However, I did hold one meeting with five of the senior players, Ieuan Evans, Will Carling, Brian Moore, Peter Winterbottom and Dean Richards, to discuss how things might pan out.

There was going to be no hiding place from the Press and therefore we had to ensure that we were a tight-knit group who got on well, and that there would be few differences of opinion. I think that, by and large, I have never been involved in a team that has had arguments or could not get on with one another. I can never understand a group of people being unable to achieve that, simply because, in all my rugby days, I have never come across a bad team spirit in any team or squad I have been associated with.

You hear stories of rifts among touring parties, like the Lions in New Zealand in 1966 and 1977, which I find difficult to comprehend. That certainly did not apply to the 1993 Lions, who were a very honest group of people. I am, however, certain that the team would have been picked differently on returning from the tour from the one that actually went. You simply do not know how people are going to react when they are on the other side of the world, away from their loved ones, their comfort zones, their work, their house and home environment, and their family life. You find out an awful lot about each other on a Lions tour and you discover those you want to go to the front with. You also establish their value as a rugby player to the Nth degree.

At the end of the 1993 Lions tour, it was very clear that we had two teams. There were those who were highly committed and extremely capable, and the others who were just lacking a wee bit in the hardness and the desire to go out there and show New Zealanders what British Rugby was capable of. It was a fascinating experience and I am sure that everyone who went on tour was the richer for it. To me, that is what playing top-level rugby is about. It is not playing in front of your home crowd or 50,000 people at Murrayfield; if you really want to test yourself, the place to do it is New Zealand, because as far as I am concerned, it is the hardest place I know to play rugby. There are no easy games in New Zealand, the pressure is intense, there is no hiding place and you just have to get on with it. It was a great credit to the Lions that we came to the third and deciding Test Match with the series squared at one-each. The highlight of the tour, from our point of view, was the second Test victory in Wellington, but it was extremely difficult, looking back, to raise our game to that level two weeks in a row.

I am putting the cart before the horse, so let us go back to the beginning of the tour. We had a successful build-up in the first four games leading up to the trauma of the Otago game. Although North Auckland and North Harbour were comparatively easy wins, our game against the New Zealand Maoris was the usual hostile battle royal. They are a real warrior race and you can clearly see the great influence they have on New Zealand Rugby, and why it is played with such ferocity. In the first half, the Maoris were threatening to overrun us and they took the lead with two excellent tries, leaving us with a huge hill to climb, because two tries, two conversions and two penalties had us 20 points down. It could have been worse for just on half-time the Maoris unleashed a tremendous counter-attack and only some desperate tackling, particularly by Dewi Morris, saved us from going 27–0 down, which would have been a point of no return.

We pulled our socks up in the second half, after I had told the side at half-time to concentrate on winning possession, but although we had gained control after 20 minutes, we only had a penalty goal to show for it. Happily, however, then came two brilliant pieces of play from Ieuan Evans, which proved what a great player he is. First he scored a brilliant try when he left his wing and the full back for dead, and then he initiated a move which put our backs on the attack to create an overlap and a try for Rory Underwood. I managed to convert both and it was now 20–17 with ten minutes to go. Stuart Barnes next switched play cleverly down the blind side, where I charged into the line to sell a dummy, and cut inside two defenders and through the full back's tackle for the winning try, which I converted. The Maoris had taught us some valuable lessons, particularly in the scrummage where they come in so hard, and they also taught us that we must go into the ruck much harder. We had discovered that this was not the Five Nations but tough southern hemisphere rugby.

Our next match was against that formidable province, Canterbury, and in another hard game we had to weather more early storms, before wresting control to win the game. We then came to the trauma of the Otago match, which we lost by 37–24. Our problem was that Otago opened the game out at every opportunity and we simply failed to react. They scored tries from what seemed innocuous situations, by sheer effrontery, and both Stu Forster and Steve Bachop were magnificent, catalysing all five tries. We suffered the biggest defeat ever inflicted on the Lions by a Provincial side and it did our morale no good at all leading up to the first Test. However, our 34–16 win over Southland picked us up a bit.

The first Test defeat at Christchurch, when we lost 18–20, was not only a bitter disappointment, but it could also have had profound repercussions due to our anger and the damage to our morale by some appalling decisions by the referee. Although Ian McGeechan had prepared us extremely well, we were a little nervous and made far too many unforced errors. Having chosen to play with the wind in the first half, it was disastrous to find ourselves five points down in the opening two minutes of the match because of an extremely controversial try. Grant Fox had kicked high to the corner where Ieuan Evans caught it, and Frank Bunce, arriving almost simultaneously, wrapped his hands around the ball, as well as Ieuan. Both players fell, holding the ball between them, but although Ieuan never let go his grip on the ball the referee, from a long way off, awarded a try. It would have been an unmitigated disaster at any stage of the game but in the opening two minutes of a first Test against the All Blacks it was catastrophic. Encouragingly, the Lions recovered and we took the lead with two penalties, but then, before half-time, Fox kicked two for the All Blacks and I kicked another, to leave the All Blacks leading 11–9. There was also much controversy surrounding our first penalty, as Michael Jones held Will Carling by the jersey without the ball. Had Michael Jones not taken out Carling, then he would surely have been on hand to take Guscott's pass and score between the posts, which would have meant a difference of four more points.

In the second half the Lions played some of their best rugby of the tour and the forwards, in particular, produced a truly valiant effort. Dean Richards, Ben Clarke and Peter Winterbottom were tremendous and inspirational, while Martin Bayfield did remarkably well in the physical rough and tumble of the line-out, not giving an inch and winning his share of quality possession. Apart from that disputed try at the start, the All Blacks never really threatened to score and our defence was excellent. With just ten minutes to go, we took the lead at 18–17 and we looked clear winners. However, throughout the game one always had a sense of doubt concerning the refereeing of Brian Kinsey from Australia, and he is certainly not going to be on my Christmas card list. We felt that once New Zealand got themselves into a kickable position, he was always going to award a penalty.

I will never forget the look of disbelief on Dewi Morris's face when he awarded that final penalty against a completely blameless Dean Richards. Fox kicked the goal from 45 yards, which was a cruel injustice, and the whistle went for full-time. It was a crushing disappointment, one of the worst of my life, because I believe that, after the way we played in the second half, we had thoroughly deserved to win that critical first Test. We felt that New Zealand were going to get better and we had calculated that the first Test was our best chance of getting into a winning position for the rest of the series, so such a robbery left us feeling pretty low for a while.

After an easy win against Taranaki, we then went on to play Auckland in what everybody regarded as the fourth Test. I got carted off with a hamstring injury before half-time, and we went down 23–18, with the remarkable Fox again kicking most of his goals. We found ourselves in the disheartening situation of suffering three consecutive Saturday defeats. To make matters worse, we went on to Hawke's Bay, where the midweek side got badly beaten on the Tuesday before the second Test, and that was undoubtedly the lowest point of the tour. A number of the guys were injured, myself included, and I was not sure if I would be fit enough to play in the second Test. The team against Hawke's Bay had performed really badly and morale at this stage was very, very low.

Raising the spirits of my team was all the more difficult because I was injured, but I told them that it was all a question of knuckling down. The team for the second Test was not announced until the Thursday afternoon, because I was not sure of my fitness and there was the question of playing Scott Gibbs in place of Will Carling. There was a doubt concerning my ability to get on to the field and I believe Geoff Cooke wanted to keep a position open for Will Carling, because of his captaincy experience, in case I did not make it.

Finally, the team was announced, with me being named although I was getting physiotherapy treatment around the clock. I went out on the Friday and I remember that all the tour supporters, about 600 of them, had come out to see us. It was a nice morning, a bit damp under foot, and we jogged three lengths around the posts; I thought, 'There is no way I can play tomorrow', because I could feel my hamstring niggling away. So I went up to Ian McGeechan, with all the photographers and their huge lenses focused on me, and said, 'Geech, look, I won't be able to play in this game tomorrow.' Firmly he said, 'You are playing tomorrow.' So we called in Geoff Cooke and Dick Best, and I repeated my doubts, but again Geech said, 'Look, I don't care if you come off after two minutes, you are going on to the field.' So I said, 'Okay, to blazes with it, I'll lead the team out.' I then gave a Press conference, with the reporters asking why I was not practising goal kicking. I said, 'You will notice the ground is very wet under foot and very muddy. Athletic Park will be completely different and it will be firm, so there's no point in my kicking today.' Basically, I bluffed and flannelled my way through the Press conference, and everyone accepted that I was going to play, although they may not actually have believed it.

During the game I could still feel my hamstring, so I decided to play myself in gently. When we were awarded a few free kicks, I got Rob Andrew to take them to touch and eventually I had a couple of penalty kicks at goal. I missed the first two, which was not really surprising as I had not been able to practise for the whole week. After that, I put a couple over, just before half-time, and all of a sudden, having been on the field for over half an hour, I had gained in confidence and knew I was going to stay on for the whole game.

I had won the toss and Geech and I had decided previously that, because of an incredibly bright sun, we would take the dangerous decision of playing into the wind and the sun. We both felt that it would probably be the best way to get the team to focus themselves and it worked, for the Lions concentrated and played some great rugby into the elements. Our forwards easily won the line-out battle and one of our most important tactical decisions was that, instead of kicking for touch, we would keep the ball in play. This, together with the fact that we put the All Black scrum under pressure, was crucial.

The only problem in the first half came when Grant Fox put up a Garryowen and, standing on my goal line, I lost the ball in the sun. Eroni Clarke got the bounce, which beat Scott Gibbs, Rory Underwood and Dean Richards, all of whom had got back in support, and he scored for Fox to convert – the Lions were trailing 7–0 after 30 minutes. The All Blacks never scored again and it said a great deal for our discipline that we never gave away a single penalty for Fox to turn into points. He had not failed to kick a single penalty in any Test match for five years, so that was some achievement. Having missed my first two penalties, one of which hit the post, I made no mistake with my next two, and just before half-time Martin Bayfield won a line-out, and Morris' fast pass gave Rob Andrew the opportunity of dropping a superb left-footed goal.

Early in the second half I kicked a third penalty, before we scored a corking try from a blistering counter-attack. Dewi Morris began it by seizing on a dropped pass inside his own half. He made the break and, straightening up, gave it to Jeremy Guscott who, with his incredible ability to inject pace, beat Frank Bunce and forced John Kirwan to check. He now flicked on to Rory Underwood, who tore up the touch line, past John Timu, for a superlative and spectacular try in the corner. If only his dive for the line had been as good as his 50-metre sprint! I kicked another penalty goal and we had actually given the All Blacks as big a hiding as they probably have ever had at home, or anywhere else for that matter. Nobody ever scores millions of points against the All Blacks, but that 20–7 victory was the most points that the Lions ever scored in a Test match against them.

I came off the field on a huge high and went up to Geech and gave him a big kiss. I said, 'Thanks to you I was part of a great experience and, if I'd called off the day before, I would have regretted it for the rest of my life.' He said, 'I knew you'd make it and that you would be all right.' It is a funny thing but in the heat of a moment and with the adrenalin flowing, you can get through. I suppose the damage was less to the hamstring than it was to my mind.

I was extremely proud of my team, particularly Rob Andrew, who had the game of his life. Few people realise how brave he is and how many tackles he puts in during the course of a game. Dewi Morris, too, had an immense game and Rory's try in the corner was one of his most memorable – and he has certainly had a few of those. Although it was the backs who put the points on the board, perhaps the real heroes, as ever, were the forwards who, to a man, were quite immense. For the rest of their lives they can say that they saw off an All Black pack in a Test match in New Zealand, which is just about as good as you can ever get. That night we were happy guys and we had a huge celebration.

We were soon to come down to earth, for in the week building up to the last Test we had one of the hardest Provincial matches of the tour against Waikato, who the previous season had won the First Division Championship and the following year were to take the Ranfurly Shield from Auckland. Obviously we had to play our second team, the Dirt Trackers. Many of them were injured and normally would not have played. However, it was felt to be extremely important that they played and remained on the field to prevent the senior team from getting a kicking and being injured in the week of the crucial third Test. Richard Webster played with a badly damaged arm and Will Carling was not fully fit, but nevertheless he played really well that day. Waikato are a very, very good team and are a huge side with massive forwards.

That day there was a lot of criticism of Scotland's front five forwards, and many people thought that they did not justify their selection for the tour. Yet beforehand few people criticised the choices. Much of the attack on them was unwarranted and unfair, for, after all, New Zealand is a hard place for forwards. So they got clattered for the biggest defeat of the tour, 38–10, but much of the blame for this lies with those who sanctioned such a fixture in the week of the final Test, or agreed the whole fixture list of the tour. It is a mystery to me that those who arrange such tours fail to consult senior players and coaches, who know what to expect and what touring in countries such as New Zealand, Australia and South Africa is all about.

If there was one team capable of raising their game after a very poor performance in the second Test, capable of wiping out the memory and getting on with a new game plan, then inevitably it would be the All Blacks. Geech and I were despairing, as our Press confidently talked of the great achievement, by a British Lions side in New Zealand, of coming back from losing the first Test and winning the series. We said to the team, 'Whatever you do, don't listen, and clearly understand that the All Blacks will be relentless in their pursuit of getting things right.' We never spoke truer words.

We started off extremely well in the third Test, with Scott Gibbs scoring a try under the post, which I converted, preceded by a penalty, which gave us a ten-nil lead. The All Blacks proceeded to play like men possessed by their great fear of losing a Test series at home, while we failed to raise our game for a second time in eight days. From then on we made critical errors, gave away penalties and it became one-way traffic in the second half. The All Black tradition and history gives them an imperative will to play winning rugby and it came to the fore on that particular day when they played one of their best games for a long time. It is in their nature to pick themselves up and fight as though their life depended on it – which, after all, is not too far from the truth.

The Lions had trained far more comprehensively during that last week to ensure that there were no question marks over people's fitness, so it was all the more disappointing to lose that final Test. Although we gave it our best shot and went into the game with a chance of winning the Test series in New Zealand for the first time since 1971, sadly we failed at the wire. It was probably the most passionate support that the All Blacks had ever received, for the crowd was simply incredible. Normally, New Zealand spectators and supporters are extremely reserved but on this particular occasion they were very noisy, and that obviously helped to inspire their players.

The man of the tour was, unquestionably, our coach Ian McGeechan and there is nothing bad that anyone can say against him. He was entirely responsible for the so near success of the British Lions. Any of the players on the 1993 Lions tour, or indeed the 1989 Lions tour, can hold their heads up high because of Ian McGeechan.

Geoff Cooke was an extremely efficient and amiable manager, and an accomplished spokesperson when dealing with the media. The whole management team was excellent, but nevertheless I had the feeling that they wanted more involvement in the preparation of the team. Geoff Cooke surely wanted a more hands-on role and you could also argue that Dick Best, as assistant coach, was in a very difficult position. On a Lions tour, you need a chief coach for getting the Saturday side ready, but then, I believe, it should be the responsibility of the assistant coach to prepare the midweek side. We sadly missed a man of Donal Lenihan's calibre, who, on the 1989 tour to Australia, took over the captaincy and much of the organisation of the Dirt Trackers, to such marvellous effect that the midweek side was always a force to be reckoned with.

Amongst the players, it was Ben Clarke who most captured the imagination and earned the admiration of all New Zealanders. We played him in three different back row positions and he was accomplished in every one. He came home an immense player, to rank alongside those other greats, Dean Richards and Peter Winterbottom. Martin Bayfield had great moments and Martin Johnson, who came on tour as a Test contender, made the grade by playing a key role in the second Test, and also playing well in the third, and I rate him very highly. Nick Popplewell was a terrific competitor, a real character and a very funny bloke. Brian Moore takes his rugby very seriously and you have to admire him for the competitiveness of his play. He is a good man to have around in a tough situation and he proved his character by forcing his way back into the side after being dropped for the first Test. I respect him highly as a player. Jason Leonard also had a great tour and showed his adaptability by swopping from loosehead to tighthead prop after the first Test.

Moving on to the backs, I think that Ieuan Evans was the equivalent of Ben Clarke, and played mightily throughout the tour. Without question, he was the pick of our backs. He scored some scorching tries and always showed himself as a highly dangerous try scorer and potential match winner. He, too, applied himself very well, took his rugby very seriously and was a hell of a good guy. He was always able to enjoy himself and he is one of the best rugby players of our time, as well as being a fine leader. Rob Andrew was the ultimate competitor, who had a huge presence on the field, and there was nothing better than his performance in the second Test. His scrum half, Dewi Morris, was another determined, combative player who never, at any time, gave up and who initiated so many fiery moves, and he, too, excelled.

Scott Gibbs also commands the greatest of respect. He played with both aggression and composure and thoroughly merited his selection for the second and third Tests and I feel that he would have played in the first had he not been injured. He is a modern-

121

day rugby player, not tall, but he is built like a brick you-know-what, very strong, very powerful in the upper body, and very quick over 15 or 20 yards. I thought him an extremely talented player. Alongside him, Jeremy Guscott has so much flair and genius that at times he is unbelievable. His silky pace is out of this world. It was beautiful to see him in full flight, but I think that on tour he lacked a bit of consistency, which was a shame, for when you watch Jeremy you are always hoping for that little bit more. When it does not materialise you are disappointed. Nevertheless, that is the nature of the man and not a criticism. He has so much natural talent as a runner and as a brilliant passer of the ball; he also tackles and kicks well and he showed all those qualities in New Zealand. Jeremy is a fine man and I enjoyed his company, and, whatever he says, I am still a better golfer than he is.

Will Carling, in his authorised biography, written by David Norrie, complains that I did not involve him in any team or captaincy decisions. Well, I suppose that is fair comment! You go about captaincy in your own way. There is a world of difference between playing rugby in your own country, in front of your own fans, and playing on the other side of the world. Past reputations count for nothing on a Lions tour and this one was no exception. You are selected for a Test side on your performances in the games leading up to it and if people fail then they are not going to be selected. It is as simple as that. Will played in one Test, but he may not have if Scott Gibbs had been fit. I think Will might be the first to admit that he did not play well on tour.

It was a difficult situation, to have such a successful England captain under my command, but I was not going to make any greater concessions to him than anyone else. If he did not want to speak to me, then that was up to him and I was not going to lose any sleep over it. I was captain of the tour and I was happy that my personal performances merited my selection for the Test matches. I wonder what would have happened if Will had been captain and whether, after the way he played, he could have justified his automatic selection. It is very difficult to drop yourself as captain of a touring side but, fortunately, I was not in that position. It is no criticism of him if you exclude him, because you pick the team from those who are playing well and deserve selection. Considering he was not at his best, then, he had no divine right to be in the Test team and I am sure no-one would argue against that philosophy.

The Wade Dooley affair was another *cause celebre* during the

122

tour. It was an appalling, incomprehensible and insensitive piece of misjudgment by the Tours Committee of the Four Home Unions. We had just arrived at Invercargill, which is about as far away from home as you can get in the southern hemisphere, when we heard that Wade's father had died, so immediately arrangements were made to fly home the extremely popular English lock. I wrote him a note of condolence, which also basically said what a great player he was and how sad it was to say goodbye to him now, but if he felt like coming back then we would love to have him, and I thanked him for his tremendous efforts on the players' behalf. The next thing we heard was that he wanted to come back, and Geoff Cooke said, 'Wade's on the flight tomorrow and he'll be with us by Saturday.' After the Auckland defeat we needed such a boost and we thought we would get that with the return of the big man. Then, all of a sudden, we heard that he was not coming and we wanted to know the reasons why. As far as I am aware, I know the door was left open by the New Zealand Rugby Union and, although we had Martin Johnson out as a replacement, they were prepared, because of the exceptional circumstances, to welcome Wade back into the touring party.

I understand the reason the Tours Committee refused to allow Wade to return was that the tour agreement was only for 30 players and if that was broken then a precedent would be set for all future rugby tours. I would question their humanity, for how often does someone's father die while he is away on tour? The Tours Committee handled the affair very badly and what they should have done was to tell Wade from the very beginning that he could not go back to New Zealand as a player. Instead, he was left to agonize and he must have had many words with his mother, his wife and his children before coming to a decision. In my view, the Committee did not show a necessary level of intelligence or compassion. In fact, what they did say to Wade was that he could return to New Zealand but he would not be allowed to play. How realistic and practical was that offer?

The Lions were so incensed by the whole affair that Bob Weighill, the secretary of the Tours Committee, who, after all, was only a spokesman, got it in the neck from the Lions party when he arrived in New Zealand shortly after the decision was made to refuse Wade's reappearance. Consequently, he and Geoff Cooke were barely speaking to each other and the Lions kangaroo court had instituted a fine on anyone caught talking to Weighill. It was a very sad and silly affair, which only showed up the dark side of the Committee of the Four Home Unions, who made the stupid decision. They were also responsible for that crazy Lions itinerary in the first place. It was the toughest tour itinerary that any touring party has undertaken, and how they ever accepted it I simply do not know. It is high time they consulted previous tour managements and senior players on all these matters, prior to accepting any such itinerary in the future.

I do not think that it affected our morale, but we certainly felt for Wade. It merely gave us players something to bitch about at a low moment of the tour. Looking back, I do not believe it was anything other than an excuse to vent our frustration at a difficult time when we were far from home. It was all the more irritating as the senior players felt that we were being commercially exploited without any compensation or remuneration. I am forced to say that, from a commercial viewpoint, the whole of the Lions tour was a disaster and, again, the Four Home Unions Committee certainly showed all their naivety when it came to negotiating the various contracts for the supply of team kit and other deals.

To go from saying that the Lions jersey was sacrosanct, with regard to commercial logos, and then suddenly agreeing the appearance of the Nike logo, with its widespread exposure, at no cost to that company, with the exception of supplying the playing and training kit, was beyond belief! They have four years between Lions tours to negotiate such deals, and why they are always left to the last minute is incomprehensible and indicative of amateur administrators handling a game which is now extremely commercial and big business.

Apart from these disappointing aspects of the tour, we still managed to have a marvellous time and we forged many friendships, even though there is not much room for pleasure on such a short and congested tour. The shorter the tour the more intense it becomes. You train most days, travel two days a week, play matches on two days a week. You have injuries to overcome, then there are team meetings and extra preparation and training to cope with, so there is little time to go out and embrace the country you are touring. However, we managed to do something fairly exciting about once a week, like clay pigeon shooting or jet-boating near Christchurch, which is a unique New Zealand activity, with jet-propelled boats skimming very fast over shallow water, giving you a surge of adrenalin and a good buzz.

During our stay at Invercargill we had a rest day and Rory Underwood, Peter Winterbottom, Paul Burnell, Ieuan Evans and I sought alternative entertainment. We chartered a plane to fly us from Invercargill to Queenstown in the Southern Alps. From the airport we took a helicopter to the top of the mountain where, instead of taking the gondola lift down, four of us decided upon an alternative form of descent, called Tandem Parapenting. You simply run off the side of the mountain, under a huge rectangular parachute, take off and come down about three thousand feet over Queenstown. It was an unbelievable and wonderful experience, but one which I almost missed. There were only three places available, with five of us going for them. Paul Burnell and I picked the short straws, so we went to see a film about Queenstown. When we came out, this guy came up to us and said, 'My ride has not turned up, so I can take one of you guys down.' We decided to toss a coin. Now, I had been captain three or four games into the tour and lost every single call, calling tails on every occasion, so I figured this time it just had to be tails. I called, and it was – I won. It was the best toss that I had won all tour.

Basically you run down the mountainside with a guy behind you, strapped into the chute, and you just take off with the wind filling the sail. He is flying and piloting the thing and lands you in the centre of Queenstown. I am quite sure that the management would have had kittens had they seen us and, as it was, I made the most ungainly landing and twisted my ankle, which required extensive physiotherapy treatment for a day or two. James Robson, our dedicated team doctor, and our marvellous physiotherapist, Kevin Murphy, were not very happy. My ankle was all blown up and pretty sore.

I think the fact that James Robson has dual qualification as a physiotherapist, as well as a doctor, helped enormously and it took a lot of the strain off Kevin Murphy. Milton Floyd, the bags man we first encountered with Scotland in 1990, was our baggage man and he was also very good on the rubs and helped with the massage. The three of them worked extremely well together and we could not have asked for better medical backup. They were really exceptional people, both in their work and in their pleasant personalities.

One of my daily chores was meeting the Press, who stood every day on the side of the pitch watching our training sessions. Their first question would invariably be, 'How did the training go today?', and we would say, 'Well, were you not actually watching?' Some of them would ask the most innocuous and stupid questions but Ian McGeechan was very good with them. As long as the Press do not hassle the players all the time, then they are not too bad, but some of them are always fishing for a story, always trying to get a different angle and to outdo one another. They are basically like a bunch of ferrets; they rarely go anywhere on their own, they are always together and they tend to feed off each other.

If people say, 'You didn't do much on the Lions tour', I reply that I was not there to do much except to play rugby and that it is your performance on the field which is going to be written about. If you are going to play rugby anywhere in the world you may as well go to New Zealand because there you are being tested against the best. If you want to go on holiday, go to Malaysia or the Caribbean. You certainly do not go on holiday on a Lions tour, you go there to play rugby, purely and simply. If you do not want to play rugby, then do not go on a Lions tour.

I have little criticism of the country. Some people accuse New Zealand of being closed all the time and that it is boring, with nothing much to do. I think New Zealand has changed a heck of a lot, certainly from when I first went there back in 1987, to my most recent visit. The hotels are very much better and they have all the modern facilities. Recreation is very high on a New Zealander's list and I would like to go back and see the country in the full glory of its summertime, because I can imagine it must be absolutely beautiful.

I do not suppose we forged great friendships with the All Black players themselves. It was more mutual respect than friendship because of the intensity and the level of competition that we were engaged in. I think that perhaps the mutual respect will transform and bloom into friendship once the playing days are over. I can say that I would be very happy to have a meal with most of them any time they care to come over to Edinburgh. It is always a marvellous experience visiting someone else's country and meeting and having a beer with people who have an outlook and environment different from your own. We made a lot of friendships on the tour, but perhaps not as many as we would have liked.

Some people have expressed the view that Lions tours should be done away with and that only individual countries should tour. I would never agree and I do not think that Lions tours are a thing of the past. If anything, they are the way forward. Touring with the Lions is a totally different experience from touring with your country, for there is great charm in the amalgam of the best players of the four Home Unions. I have an argument that you should increase the regularity of Lions tours, for I simply do not see why you have to tour only once every four years. Over an eight-week period you build up a team spirit, a pattern of play, a sense of well-being and all that goes with it, and then all of a sudden it is ended abruptly.

By comparison, the All Blacks, the Wallabies and the South Africans have the advantage of continuity by constantly touring. Why do the Lions not tour two years consecutively and then have a four-year gap? You could then achieve some continuity because approximately two-thirds of your players would remain constant. You would identify and reject the failures, thus strengthening the tour party for the second tour. One year you could go to New Zealand and the following year to South Africa; four years later it may be Australia and then New Zealand, and we could mix it up a bit. It is time, too, to argue a case for going to Canada and Argentina, but there is no doubt in my mind that you are always going to have your strongest tours to New Zealand and South Africa. Australia has only two strong Provincial sides and once you have played them and Australia there is no one else to play in a meaningful game. In New Zealand and South Africa you play top Provincial sides week in, week out. The problem with the shorter, eight-week tour is that midweek you play some of the top Provincial sides that you used to play on Saturdays, which makes it tougher. What you are actually doing is being given a tour without an easy game, which makes it much harder to go through undefeated against the Provincial teams.

However it is difficult to advocate anything longer than the present 13-match tour in the current economic situation, which makes jobs thin on the ground. Nowadays you simply could not get away with longer tours. It remains essential to have a few relatively easy games on tour in order to have a breather and to sort yourselves out, especially between Test matches.

It was a fabulous honour to captain the British Lions in New Zealand, for I like the country and I respect New Zealand rugby players. At the same time, I would like to think that they respect me as a rugby player because I performed at a level in New Zealand that I am proud of, and I am similarly proud of the way that the Lions performed in the Test Series. We held our heads high, we conducted ourselves well, both on and off the field, and you cannot hope for, or expect, anything more than that.

CHAPTER IX

Under the High Ball

THERE IS ALWAYS a divergence of opinion as to what constitutes the various qualities players need in different positions. The French might say that there is too much consideration given to specialisation and that everyone should have a broad range of all-round capabilities. I feel, however, that the full back position requires a temperament all of its own because, as the last line of defence, it is a very exposed situation.

All of us would agree that the full back should be a sure fielder, a good kicker with either foot and a deadly tackler, with the timing and the speed to launch either a counter-attack or take his place in a rehearsed or impromptu move; but which quality would we select as being the most important?

Full back play is first and foremost about defence and therefore I believe that is the most significant quality. After all, you are known as being the last-ditch defender, and that is often how you are judged. You have to develop an instinct to read the game that is being played out in front of you. I do not think that anyone has ever, at any time, told me where I should stand in any given situation, and therefore I have depended upon long experience and an instinct for anticipation, which is only gradually acquired. I have never been one of the quickest rugby players in the world, but I have had the ability to read a game and anticipate my role in defence and attack.

First and foremost, the full back must be totally secure under the high ball, but then he must also be a strong tackler and have the ability, in many ways, to act like a goalkeeper in soccer and to marshal and control the three-quarter line of his own team. Communication is vital in defence and in any part of attack, and the full back has to be able to control what his three-quarter line will do in any given situation. There is no doubt that you can give a great deal of confidence to your forwards when the opposition put up a high ball if your pack are fairly sure that you are going to catch cleanly and kick safely to touch with either foot, or call for a mark, or indeed set up a counter-attack. Every situation is different and requires a separate response.

A safe pair of hands is probably the first requisite of the full back, for if he misses and knocks on, the effect on the morale of the rest of the team and the feeling of insecurity that is created can be devastating.

Whenever the opposition puts up a high kick in my direction, I know instinctively whether I am going to have to jump in the air to catch that ball, or have time to mark it, or, indeed, have time to gather and run. Nobody can teach you that, you simply have to have a sense of where the opposition are, how high the ball has gone and whether you have the time. There is often an occasion in a game when the ball comes to me at full back, inside my own 22, and I have plenty of time to make a mark but I do not see the point. If you catch the ball and know that you have got four or five yards in which to react and move, then it may be that there is something more available, such as a counter-attack. Too often you see full backs just calling for the mark unnecessarily and taking the free kick, which is certainly a safe option, but so unimaginative.

Kicking ability is second to the value of safe fielding, but accuracy in finding touch or, nowadays, putting the ball where you want it in order to avoid lines-out, is essential. With the wind behind you, the high kick can rarely be too high, for the higher the ball the more difficult it will be for the other team to catch it unopposed, and there will be more time for your forwards or backs to get underneath it if you have managed to follow up yourself and put them onside. Similarly, against the wind it is better to use a shallow trajectory. Another important point is that the cleaner you can take the ball, the quicker you will be able to do something with it. Never take your eyes off the ball, even fractionally, to look at the oncoming opponents.

There is no hard and fast rule where you should stand, for the position is always changing with the circumstance, but commonsense rules apply. If playing against the wind, you stay well back and, if you are in a howling gale, you stand still further back. Another objective is to look after your own forwards and, at the same time, try to tire out the opposition. You must be careful not to dally too long, for then there is a risk of a charge down and, if this is the case, it is always far better to hang on and face the music than to allow the opportunity of a score by the opposition.

The qualifications for full back play, fielding, kicking to touch, punting off either foot, tackling and counter attacking, can only be perfected by practice and then more practice.

There is no doubt that in modern International rugby there is always a lot of pressure imposed by high kicks to the opposition by both teams in the opening exchanges, in order to test their respective defence. A lot of the first-phase possession is simply pumped high into the air by either the half back or the stand off. You therefore have to ensure that early in the game you can cope with it and give your forwards the reassurance which is so psychologically comforting. I repeat, the wind will affect where you stand and you have to take every single factor into account. I used to rush and, if balls had gone over the dead ball line, I would race to grab them and try and take quick 22 drop outs. However, I have learned over the years to read a game more effectively and understand that if you are under a period of sustained pressure, you simply have to slow everything down and settle in order to gradually get back into the game.

If you, as a full back, are going to rush a drop-out when your side is having problems, you merely keep the pressure on your own team and that does not help anybody. It is, therefore, essential to be constantly reading the game and I feel the full back has a better opportunity than most to survey the ebb and flow in front of him, and to play a major part in a team's decision-making. Often you do not have that much time to think – you have to rely more on instinct and to sense what is going on around you. You have to rely sometimes on your wings coming back to help you in defensive situations and, as I have said, communication is a crucial part of one's game. I always try to work in close harmony with my wings, in much the same way as two cricketers at the crease are constantly calling and speaking to each other at all times.

As a kid I remember seeing JPR Williams, who had a great love of physical contact and a total disregard for his own personal safety, as a tremendously aggressive tackler. He was not as big as me but he could certainly cream out the biggest All Black forward.

I also remember Bruce Hay, who played a number of times on the wing and at full back for Scotland, as well as going on two Lions tours in 1977 and 1980. Bruce was a tremendous tackler against any opposition – always extremely strong, he would really scythe them down. Both these full backs were extremely brave under the high ball, and they had some of the qualities that I have always tried to emulate in my years as a full back.

Another defensive attribute of the full back is the shepherding of the attacker into tight corners. I think that a good winger will always beat a full back, if he has acres of room to spare, because of sheer pace, but a good full back can make up for this by forcing them towards the touch lines, which they can use as an extra defender.

The counter-attack is one of the great attractive ploys in any full back's game and there were probably no better exponents of the art than that silky runner, Serge Blanco of France, or Scotland's own Andy Irvine, whose acceleration and searing speed was such that he would certainly leave me for dead. Both these players were blessed with astonishing pace, for which there is no substitute, especially when you are coming from full back and you have the opportunity to run from deep inside your own half or from any passage of broken play. We saw the number of fantastic tries that Blanco scored for France based on this quality, although he was also blessed with a supreme confidence. I think his aplomb came from that underlying attribute of his game, as did Andy Irvine's. I could never hope to compare myself with either of those fine players in attacking terms, simply because they had so much pace.

I think that my role as a full back has always been to try and be a compromise between the best attacking and the best defensive players. By and large, I believe that I have probably achieved that, although I would never say that I was as strong as Bruce Hay or JPR in defence, or have the same presence in attack as Irvine and Blanco. Nonetheless, as an all-rounder I think that perhaps I have been a good compromise of all the different qualities required. In the same way, I do not think that JPR or Bruce Hay matched me in attack, nor could Irvine or Blanco compare with me in the defensive mould.

You have to make the most of your attributes and, as a big man, six foot two and 14½ stone, running like the wind was never natural or easy for me. I think the closest counterpart to me as a full back, that I saw, was Roger Gould of Australia. He was a big man in every sense of the word and a tremendously influential player in that great Wallaby side of 1984, which made the Grand Slam against our four Home Unions. I could only admire him from afar because I never had the opportunity to play against him, but I can now relate to what he was trying to do when he played rugby. So much of Australia's attack, at that time, centred around Gould, who was used in many cases as the pivot, with Ella and Campese working off him.

I always admired Paul Thorburn of Wales, and I thought he was a much better rugby player than he was ever given credit for. I think it was one of the great losses to Welsh Rugby when Paul decided to hang up his boots after captaining Wales through some troubled times, particularly that disastrous tour to Australia in 1991. Not only was Paul a very good attacking player, but he was a magnificent kicker and, of course, we Scots will never forget the record 70-yard and eight-inch penalty that he kicked against us at Cardiff. I think it took Wales a few years before they found anybody capable of replacing Paul Thorburn and even now they are still toying with a couple of players and have never really found an adequate replacement, good footballers that Tony Clement and Mike Rayer undoubtedly are.

Some of the recent England full backs, Jonathan Webb, Simon Hodgkinson and Jonathan Callard, are all much of a muchness, and they gave me the impression of a certain fragility in defence, yet no one could ever accuse them of not performing effectively in an England jersey. I feel that a full back needs to have an aura of imposing stature and presence on the field, which makes the opposition aware that he could be a dangerous player. I do not believe that these guys had these attributes.

For the best of the more contemporary full backs, you have to look overseas to men like John Gallagher of New Zealand. He went into the All Black team in the World Cup year of 1987 and simply played magnificently, scoring some sensational tries which were mostly achieved by his brilliant appreciation of angles of running, of which he was the finest exponent that I have ever seen. It was all about the timing of his run and his injection of pace. Serge Blanco was an inspirational player who lived more off his wits than other people. Gallagher was a more technical player who did everything with such precision that I believe that he would still have been playing full back for New Zealand in 1994 if he had not turned professional and gone to Rugby League where, strangely, he never fitted in and failed to set the world on fire. I found it very sad to see such a talented player not making the grade in Rugby League, but perhaps that simply shows how tough and how fickle Rugby League can be, when very talented Rugby Union players go over and try to make their mark in the different professional code. Everyone makes their choice, and John Gallagher chose to try and make it in the League game. It is probable that he now has a few pounds in the bank, but little else in terms of personal satisfaction, apart from what he achieved with the All Blacks. I wonder, if he had his time over again, whether he would make the same decision. Personally, I doubt it.

Just as Wales have never found another JPR, so Australia have never found another Roger Gould. They had Greg Martin for a while and then Marty Roebuck, whose style was reminiscent of some of the English full backs I have mentioned, in that he never seemed entirely secure under the high ball. Yet he did his job pretty well, scored some good tries and was an excellent goal kicker. Similarly, New Zealand never found an adequate substitute for Gallagher. Kieran Crowley tried to fill his shoes for a couple of seasons and then they converted John Timu from wing to full back, but I still do not believe that he provides the complete answer.

I repeat, I think that people will regard me as being a good all-round full back, without the inspiring attacking flair of some, nor indeed the deadly defence of others, such as my brother Scott, who has always been a truly great tackler and defender. No position is more exposed than full back, for if you miss a tackle or drop a high ball everyone sees you and it is impossible to be anonymous. If you make a similar mistake at stand off, at centre or in the forwards, there are usually numerous people and opportunities to quickly cover up. There is no doubt that the full back is the most visible person on a rugby field and his mistakes tend to be exaggerated because he is so exposed.

The drift defence is now so commonplace in International rugby, especially off first-phase possession, that it is becoming harder and harder with each season to find a way through the opposing defence. There is also the cluttering up of the midfield by big athletic forwards. We are, therefore, struggling to think up new ideas and new moves to combat that swarm defence, at which Australia are absolute masters. Nowadays we have to put an enormous amount of preparation into our angles of running and our timing, to try and break through such well-organised defence. Prior to 1986, many tries were scored from first-phase possession, but more recently the scoring of tries from those situations is becoming a rarer and rarer experience. Instead, you just have to play for continuity of possession and it is only after the third or fourth breakdown that the gaps are going to open up to allow try-scoring opportunities.

As the name suggests, with the drift defence people tend to drift outwards all the time, and anyone coming back, cutting against the grain, will always have a chance of breaking inside the trailing arm of a tackler. It is really a question of working out the necessary angle and waiting for the opportunity. Very often it is the scissors and the coming inside on to a reverse pass that succeeds in breaking those midfield defences. An instance of that came during the recent British Lions tour, when I was able to score a try that turned out to be the winning score against the New Zealand Maoris. My brother Scott took the ball in midfield and we suddenly changed the direction of running to the blind side, where Stuart Barnes got the ball and I came in on the angle to cut inside two or three defenders to get over the try line. It showed how the continuity of possession that is so vital in modern-day rugby, and the keeping of the ball alive to allow you to switch the play and vary the angle, can crack even the most resolute defence. It does mean, however, that you have to concentrate the whole time, for in the modern game it has become far more difficult to do things off the top of your head.

It is very difficult to describe them, but there have been some amazing tries scored as a result of people both timing their runs and changing their angles of running. There are, of course, still many opportunities to come into a line on a two to two or three to three situation, or whatever, and again timing of the pass plays its part in making the extra man and allowing him to come into that line in the correct place, either between the centre and outside centre, or between the outside centre and wing, or even outside the wing. It is all about judgment and it is not only the full back himself who is responsible, but the timing of the pass to him. You rely on your centres to pass the ball at the precise split second that gets you through that vitally important half-gap. You have to be constantly reading the game, and go with the ebb and flow and rely on instinct. Sometimes you can see the ball going left and you suddenly say to yourself, 'I've got to go with this and make the extra man.' Rugby is largely based on intuitions, especially in second and third phase possessions, and you have to ensure that you are up to any changes in movement or direction, and sense where there could be an overlap situation where you have to go in and provide that extra link which achieves the overlap.

These days we are often reluctant, on first or second-phase possession, to spread the ball too wide in our own half and, therefore, I often like to come in close to the scrum to crack that middle layer of defence, but I must then make sure that my forwards are in support and provide continuity by winning the ball for the next phase. In recent years Scotland have tried to develop a pattern of play that is not overly rigid in any area of the field. I have often been involved in runs in my own half close to the forwards, which sometimes the opposition do not expect. A classic example of this came during Scotland's 1991 World Cup game against Western Samoa, in the quarter finals. We were playing the first half into a very strong breeze and to kick five or ten yards into touch was not making the best use of the ball. Therefore, the first two or three times we won from a ruck, I came very short on a pass from Gary Armstrong and drove through the middle of the Samoan forwards, which took them by surprise, and this way we launched wave after wave of attacks to take us 40 or 50 yards upfield. It showed the right sort of tactics to employ when playing into the wind, when many teams would have taken the easier option of kicking the ball into touch. The French are very good at that, and they tend to get their big back row and second row men running off into space, but always the transference of ball and its retention are extremely important.

There are no better and finer exponents than the French at giving a deep pass when other nations might give the more obvious flat pass that would just land everyone in trouble. The French are marvellous at the deep passing game and always seem to have players running hard and at real pace on to the ball. It is wonderful to see them in full flow and it is a shame that few other sides have ever attempted to copy them.

I want to go back to the importance of absolute concentration at all times by the full back, for it is really one position on the field where you cannot relax for a second. A prime example of this, which is a lesson for all budding full backs, was an incident against France during my first game for Scotland, when I turned my back on the opposition. That is something which you should never do at any time, in any match.

Scotland had won the toss and decided to kick off, and I was called on by our captain, Colin Deans, to take the kick. Unfortunately, because I was so full of adrenalin, I slightly over-hit the ball, which landed a metre or two into touch. I jogged back to take up position within my own 22, thinking that the forwards would not be very pleased with me as they made their way back to the halfway for the ensuing scrum. Suddenly, I heard the crowd beginning to roar and I turned round to see about six or seven Frenchmen bearing down on me, and one of them was holding the ball. It was a matter of eeny-meeny-miny-mo, so I picked out one target to tackle but, of course, he had passed the ball and within seconds of my International debut we were 4–0 down. I found myself saying, 'I hope that this is not what International rugby is all about.' Fortunately, matters improved and ultimately we triumphed 18–17. I had learnt one of the most valuable lessons of my career during that victory, which is never to turn your back on the opposition, and that can apply to all rugby players, no matter what position they play.

I enjoy, and make a point of, looking at the opposition stand off and the blind side wing, because sometimes, just by looking at them you can sense when the ball is going to be put back into the box as the blind side wing begins lining up fairly flat. You must always look out for hand or head signals. Prejudging where the opposing stand off is going to place the ball, by hand or by foot, is essential. The reading of what the opposing backs might do in any given situation gives the full back valuable seconds to play with.

The thing I enjoy most in a defensive situation is putting in a tremendous tackle by closing down the opposition and forcing them into the position I want them and being very aggressive in the launch. I often watch players who are reluctant in the tackle and, in contrast, those who cannot get there fast enough to make that tackle, and I know which of these players is really enjoying himself and is up for the challenge.

A great confidence booster is to make a mark under severe pressure and then put in a 40- or 50-yard kick to touch, which is almost like putting two fingers up to the opposition. You do have other mundane but vital duties, such as helping to marshal your team's defence in order to close down the opposition, while you are constantly looking for attacking options and opportunities so that you can go forward and help breach the gain line and put away the try scores. Being able to assist them in doing that gives great satisfaction and it is something that I have always thoroughly enjoyed, almost as much as scoring them myself.

Full back play means total involvement. It is not only the defensive or the attacking chores, it is having complete commitment for the whole 80 minutes of a game. You can never afford to relax and there is always something to keep your eye on. The opposition may perform a quick, long drop out, a fancy kick off or a quick throw in and if you, at any time, turn your back then you are asking for trouble. You have to be alert at all times, even when for very long periods you do not have the ball in your hands. You rarely have to go looking for work, for there is always plenty to be done. I see myself as a very good support player and when tries are being scored I am never too far away from the try scorer, for that is part and parcel of my make-up. Rugby is a 15-man game.

I am often asked about the situation when, after I have gone up in attack, something goes wrong; either the ball goes whistling over my head towards my own line, or there is a quick counter attack; in other words I get caught with my pants down. All I can say is that if we all worked on the negative aspect, then no full back would go outside his own 22. You simply have to have a sense of adventure, but you also must have confidence in your team-mates, for if you are in an attacking position and you have called a move, and there is an opportunity to attack, then you must know that somebody like the blind side wing is covering for you. You must also have the confidence that, in the attacking situation, your team will retain possession and carry through that option. Very often it is up to the full back to have a marshalling role and to encourage the others to make the most of opportunities which are open to them.

PLACE KICKING
There is nothing quite like the pressure of having to kick for goal in International rugby in front of 60,000 people, when the chips are down and you are really up against it, with an opportunity to kick a crucial goal to win the match. Penalty goals are all important in the modern game and more often than not are decisive in either winning or losing. They give your team and yourself, as the kicker, a tremendous lift when you get them over, but a feeling of a lost opportunity when you fail. Alas, I think that my career as a goal kicker may be remembered for one kick in particular, during the fateful semi-final of the 1991 World Cup, when I missed a penalty opportunity against England, with 20 minutes to go, to put the game 9–6 in Scotland's favour. It was such an easy kick and I should have got it; there is no excuse. Similarly, top golfers should always hole their two-foot putts but, when it comes down to a hell of a lot of pressure, everything seems to tighten up. All you can do in these situations is to be positive and to concentrate on your technique which has served you well in practice.

You must have a positive outlook on goal kicking, and I have always, for the last six or seven years, practised assiduously in front of the posts where I normally get 19 out of 20 successes. I usually start off at the 22-yard line and then go further out as I get more confident and more warmed up.

Goal kicking is a very individual thing and every goal kicker has his own routine. I remember watching the mercurial Lescarboura kicking for France. He used to go back two steps and just have one walk step into his kick, yet he could still hammer the ball over from 45 metres. That was when I realised that you do not need to have a really long run-up and it is that last stride into the ball which is most important. Providing you keep your head down over the ball and you concentrate on the exact spot where you are going to hit it with your foot, then you cannot go too far wrong. Seeing Lescarboura kick helped me to devise a new run-up, which I have stuck to for the last seven years. It is always three steps backwards, two to the side and a little half step back, before coming in slowly and making certain that the non-kicking, pivot foot is always planted near to the ball. You then keep your eye firmly on the ball and kick a high follow through, towards the uprights.

By and large, it has always worked for me. Of all the great kickers there has been none better than Grant Fox of New Zealand, who is a superb striker of the ball, and you see it always turning end over end as it sails between the posts. Michael Lynagh is another beautiful kicker of the placed ball and, for a short, stocky chap, he could certainly kick it a long way. Other great exponents of place-kicking were Hugo Porta of Argentina, who was an incredible place-kicker as well as a drop-kicker of the ball; Paul Thorburn of Wales, who holds the record for the longest international penalty; and Naas Botha, whom we should never discount because of his isolation in South Africa, was a wonderfully natural striker of the ball. Dusty Hare, who retired in 1984, was England's best goal kicker of the last 50 years, always remembered by the English supporters for his kicking under pressure. I recall the goal he kicked for England against Wales that set them on their way to the Triple Crown and Grand Slam in 1980, and the following year he scored all of England's 19 points at Cardiff.

All these great kickers had one thing in common, that of great rhythm. They each had their own style but always did the same things, and you could see their concentration as they teed up the ball and took their four, five or six paces back, or as in Lescarboura's case, just a couple. You develop an individual style, just like any golfer and, if it works for you, then you must stick with that style for it is vitally important to retain consistency in everything you do – that is the key for any potential goal kicker.

Keeping your eye on the ball is the infallible rule of good kicking. When, after taking the ball to make a kick, you first look at your objective, whether it is the crossbar and the uprights, or a point in touch in the case of a defensive clearance, you then adjust your stance, still looking at your objective, and finally back at the ball, from which you must never let your eyes wander till the kick has been taken. Never try to be too ambitious; a sure 30 yards is far better than a dicey 50 yards, and the greater length will come with practice and experience. When punting, never throw the ball in the air, but place it on your foot and remember to practise with both feet, for that will make you a far more valuable player.

Another important consideration in goal kicking is the taking into account of the pitch and weather conditions. The wind can play havoc with any goal kicker, as it can with any golf swing. If it is blowing in your face, you have to judge how hard and how much it limits your range; if it is coming from behind, the same thing applies, but of course it can give you a much greater range. You therefore have to decide whether it is within your range to take the kick at goal or whether it would be better to use the ball tactically, by kicking to touch or employing a Garryowen. If you are kicking into the wind, you tend to place the ball on the sand at a lower angle than if you are just hoisting it with the wind behind you. If the wind blows crossfield, again you have to judge the degree of aim off so that it comes in between the posts, usually late in its flight. These are all vital judgements which usually are made easier after long experience.

The important thing is (and here I am perhaps lucky that I have a thick skin) that, if you hit a poor kick and it does not go over, you must put it behind you and out of your mind, to ensure that the next time you approach a goal kick you are in a positive frame of mind. I find that it helps by visualising the ball going between the uprights, prior to taking the kick. You must also try to shut the crowd out of your mind and only concentrate on the techniques and the rituals that have served you time and time again; that is, placing the ball and making sure it is lined up in the correct way, and going through your normal step-back procedures. I always have two of the seams of the ball pointing towards the middle of the goal posts and I kick the ball, in the upright position, at the seam joining two panels. Some players, like Grant Fox, favour the ball being tilted slightly forward, whereas Dusty Hare always had it tilted slightly back towards him. What you must do is retain a sense of consistency in all your procedures and visualise the ball going between the posts, shutting everything out of your mind and simply concentrating on the job in hand.

It is a great feeling when the ball goes between the posts, especially with a difficult kick from a long way out, and you know you have achieved a tremendous strike. It gives not only yourself but also your team-mates enormous satisfaction and a great lift.

There are two schools of goal kicking technique; the scientific, straight toe kicker, who is a technical type of goal kicker, and the touch kicker, who kicks around the corner with the instep, and seems to be more natural. I think that the more modern kickers have tended to favour around the corner, but that has a lot to do with the development of the much lighter soccer or rugby boot worn by modern-day players. In the past, the toe kickers tended to have a hard toecap and a squared-off toe on their boots, which obviously enabled more accuracy when it came down to straight-forward, frontal toe kicking. That is changing, and many players have now perfected the round the corner technique. Provided that the same sort of consistency is retained in the run-up, then they can be just as accurate as the toe kickers.

Goal kickers win games! I will always remember Paul Thorburn kicking that superlative goal from the touchline at Rotorua to beat Australia in the dying moments and win third place in the 1987 World Cup. The contribution of Grant Fox to winning so many matches for New Zealand with his place-kicking is legendary and the same is true of Michael Lynagh, who was highly influential in winning the World Cup for Australia in 1991. To my chagrin, Jonathan Callard's marvellous pressure kick beat Scotland only last season. I, too, have had my moments, such as in the last Test in Australia in 1989, when I kicked five penalty goals, which, together with Ieuan Evan's try, was enough to win the game for the Lions.

As a goal kicker, you share in the highs as well as the lows. When you kick well, everyone comes up and congratulates you, but when you kick poorly you are really on your own. It can be tough and thankless but that is part of the individual pressures of the goal kicker. It is far removed from the rest of the game of rugby, but if you elect to become a goal kicker then you must treat your job seriously and stay out long after the others have gone in to shower, to practise, and hope that on the day your kicks will go over.

Goal kicking can be a real bitch goddess, as from experience I can recall kicking everything in sight in practice and then, in the International the next day, missing five out of six. There are other days when I have hardly kicked anything in practice but the next day have hammered them from all over the pitch. It seems to come down to how you feel on the day and how your team is doing as a whole, and is largely a question of confidence. The first couple of kicks are crucial and, therefore, the simpler they are the better. It is a damn sight easier kicking the ball from in front of the posts after a try rather than out on the touch line, and I am, therefore, often irritated when I see try-scorers not making a total effort to touch down far closer to the posts, feeling perhaps that their job is finished when they go over the line. As far as I am concerned, they should make every effort to gain every yard, so that the goal kicker has an easier job.

All the great goal kickers have their off days and even Grant Fox is not infallible. As in the analogy with golf, one day you can play well and another you cannot, for no apparent reason. The important thing is to never let it get you down, and to teach yourself that it is part of life's tribulations and remember it is only a game. Sitting in the dressing-room after my calamitous miss in that 1991 World Cup defeat by England, I distilled my failure down to the realisation that it was far from being the end of the world, and what people forget is that I scored a higher percentage of kicks that went over during the World Cup than any other goal kicker. Over the whole piece I kicked very, very well but, alas, people will tend to remember that one incident. At the end of the day, you take the chances that come your way and if you kick them that is fine, but if you miss, then no one should accuse you of not trying, not concentrating or being sufficiently committed.

CHAPTER X

Problem Areas

NO MAJOR WORLD GAME is increasing in popularity or changing at the current rate of Rugby Union Football. Such has been the acceleration of huge money into the game from sponsors, television rights and income from immense new stadia that it has brought massive new demands on both the players and the administrators. We are, therefore, involved in a very critical period of change within the world of Rugby Union, both in terms of the amateur and professional arguments and with the nature of the game itself.

If the rewards are going to be greater, will it bring a different type of animal into the sport and will it, for that reason, be a meaner spirited game? Those are questions which are difficult to answer and I often wonder whether, if I was playing for big money rather than for national pride, my attitudes would be the same, and would such factors as the professional foul creep into our game? All I know is that the game is becoming more and more popular and many more kids of both sexes are going to be attracted to the sport. It is also true that there will be significant changes within the pecking order of world rugby in the next decade.

It makes you wonder sometimes where the game has been, and why it has taken so long for the whole momentum to gather and for the resolve to appear to make rugby a truly major world game. The old-time administrator was certainly too conservative, insular and probably too conceited concerning success in the smaller pond of Europe and in the southern hemisphere. Now that we are all swimming in the big pool, largely created by the momentum generated by the 1987 and 1991 World Cups, there is a greater awareness of the need for change, particularly in regard to the exploitation of the amateur player, on whom they have heaped intolerable pressure. Something had to give and inevitably it was the amateur ethic. The World Cups provided a forum in which the players of the world got together to exchange ideas and philosophies which affected their own future, and probably accelerated the thrust towards professionalism.

The Five Nations Championship was a typical example of narrow-mindedness and, because it was so prodigiously successful, indeed a licence to print money, it insulated our administrators from the better and bigger things happening in the southern hemisphere. We were years too late getting into coaching and competitive structures and therefore our game remained stagnant and we failed to match the commitment and dedication to winning, which is a hallmark of both the New Zealanders and the Australians, not to mention South Africa.

The problem areas now facing us are the way the game is going, in patterns of play, changing laws with the emphasis on big men and power play, and whether or not it will become a flat-out professional game. It is often said that Rugby Union has despised Rugby League and made them appear the pariahs. Personally, I never felt that League carried any stigma whatever, but I could see why our administrators kept them at arm's length. It was largely a defence mechanism against the marauding cheque book which, from time to time, creamed off leading Union players, especially in a country like Wales which has a different social structure and where rugby tends to be more of a working-class game than in the rest of the British Isles. In the Eighties, they lost some of their very best players like Jonathan Davies, John Devereux, Adrian Hadley, David Young, Paul Moriarty, and others; almost three-quarters of an International team. It was no wonder that the Welsh not only lost a great deal of stature in the rugby world, but that they became paranoid and determined to staunch the bleeding from a savage wound by initiating financial schemes to hold on to their players.

Now that Rugby Union is marching down the professional road, the differences between Union and League are becoming more muted and less relevant. It is my belief that the game will shortly go professional, not only at the highest level of International Rugby but also at the club level in England and Wales and to a lesser extent Ireland. I cannot see it happening at club level in Scotland at the moment because the money or the interest is simply not there. If, however, we restructure to the provincial level, it is possible then that the Scots can be paid, which would give a greater determination to those playing at the lower level to achieve the rewards offered at the higher level.

Nowadays the administrators have put far too great a demand on individuals. These demands are much bigger than people realise, for the standard of fitness required in the modern game is colossal and the time involved is inestimable. There is also the great danger of physical injury, especially under the new laws, which, because of greater power and pace, are creating dangerous situations. Players are getting hurt due to the overpowering of forward play and the frustration and ferocity of players in certain situations, such as the necessity to win ruck ball in crucial circumstances in your opponents' 22 or under the posts.

How can you say to the modern top players, who are bringing millions and millions of pounds into their respective Rugby Unions, 'Thank you, boys, but sorry you are not getting any of it?' Now that rugby has become such a huge game world wide with a considerable following, we need to make sure that the players are properly rewarded, for nowadays they are not only sportsmen but entertainers. We are doing everything that all the other professional sportsmen are doing and therefore we must be paid for the time and effort we put in – surely, most would argue that there is nothing wrong with that?

Much of the game is now being run by professional organisations or full-time administrators whose bodies are involved in seeking sponsorship opportunities and negotiating television, broadcasting and advertising deals, so the whole game has moved at a vast pace over the past decade and will undoubtedly move even faster in the next. The next World Cup in South Africa could be the launch pad and the catalyst to send rugby into a new dimension, and we in the British Isles and Scotland, particularly, must not be left behind. Many of us thought that the first World Cup held in Australia and New Zealand in 1987 would have projected rugby very quickly into a professional age. That it did not happen was due to the conservative northern hemisphere unions, but attitudes have hardened considerably since then and even the 1991 World Cup could be small beer in comparison with the South African World Cup in 1995.

When the game does become professional then the players must realise that they will be in an entirely different ball game, and far more will be demanded from them by the general public in terms of performance and entertainment. This brings me to the problems besetting the game itself, for in the 1993/1994 season the game was certainly not what it once was in terms of providing a spectacle, and we have to look at ways of making it more attractive to the paying supporters who at the moment are being served up mediocre fare, especially in the Five Nations.

The recent law changes have altered the whole character of the game, while the build-up of gigantism can be seen amongst the world's forwards, which means that huge forwards are there on the basis of brute strength in order to control and dominate the opposition. This battering ram approach has, in my view, done the game a great disservice, for it has built up a depth of attritional defence in midfield which is beginning to prove impenetrable. The problem these days is that those big English forwards, like Martin Johnson, Tim Rodber, Martin Bayfield and Ben Clarke, and their southern hemisphere counterparts, are not only huge but are tremendous athletes – they can all shift around the field at a rate of knots which can embarrass many backs.

We now have to ask, 'What do the players and the spectators actually want from a game of rugby?' There is no doubt in my mind that they want to see tries being scored and they do not want to see so many kicks at goal. We therefore have to look at other ideas, other ways, of ensuring that far more tries are scored. At the moment the law makers are treading water, without clearly admitting or recognising that something needs to be done. The law makers on the International Board have made far too many mistakes recently, and these include increasing the try to five points, therefore giving, with the goal, a seven-point total compared with a penalty goal worth three points. This has meant that teams have deliberately and cynically conceded the penalty rather than risk having seven points scored against them, a matter which the All Blacks exploited in the UK in 1993.

To combat that, Scotland, in their experimental law changes at the end of the 1993/1994 season, changed the try from five points to three points, with one point for the conversion, so that a goaled try became four points and the penalty three in order that the differential would not be as great. This method will also serve to keep down some of the ludicrously high scores achieved when one team is often only slightly superior to another.

I still think that the penalty goal is too influential and that the laws contain far too many anomalies. For instance, how on earth

146

can they consider that a deliberate knock on is not worth a penalty? The fact that it is only a free kick is absolutely daft because, without question, it is cheating when you try and knock a ball down to prevent a try being scored. There are some other innocuous little laws, such as if you slice your kick and the ball goes up into the air and your forwards are in front of you when the ball comes down, and they have not moved out of a ten-yard circle, that is then a penalty. How you can give a penalty for that, as opposed to a free kick for a deliberate knock on, is incomprehensible. There are many ambiguities in the laws of rugby and it seems to me that little has been or is being done to try and simplify the laws of the game, for rugby, in its essence and purest form, is surely a simple game.

It is unfortunate that the laws make rugby a complicated game, and I think that we should try and strip it all away and go back to the bare essentials, say, 'What are we trying to do here?', then try and frame laws and regulations that would be easy to understand, easy to interpret and easy to play with. We should build a set of laws which are applicable to the demands of modern rugby and the new influences, such as increased fitness, more powerful physical specimens and better athletes, which were not as pertinent in the old days. I am not saying it would be an easy job, but surely there are enough intelligent people involved in world rugby who could sit down and re-write the whole of the laws of rugby football, because at the moment they are an absolute shambles.

The International Board, at the end of the 1993/1994 season, have announced that there is no change to the maul situation and, if the team taking the ball into the maul fail to feed it back, then the put-in at the scrum goes to the opposition. They have, however, announced that if a team takes a ball into the ruck and it does not come back, then, if they are going forward, they will get the put-in at the scrum. I think that, at least, will be a good thing and it will encourage teams to go back to the rucking form of the game, making the rolling maul less influential. The ruck is a dynamic, forward-moving piece of rugby, forward play at its finest, and the best exponents of this have been New Zealand over the years and Scotland under the influence of Jim Telfer. There is certainly a place for the ruck in any game of rugby.

Tragically, the rolling maul has changed the character of the game significantly in the last few years – we are now often playing a sort of glorified Eton Wall game. I find this a very boring way of playing rugby, but as a rugby player I have got to fit in with the laws. It seems to me to be crazy that these administrators who change the laws never seem to speak with the players or the coaches in order to get a consensus opinion. In order to re-design the laws, we should take coaches from the major International Rugby teams, who are presumably the best coaches in each country, at least I would like to think so, and put them in a think tank with a few top referees. The players are not necessary because the coaches will have developed their ideas in long discussions with the players on how they want to change the game. I do not believe that anything will be agreed if you have too many people around a table. I think that it is the coaches who must be ultimately responsible for the path that the game is taking and the laws which create it.

The administrators of the Laws Committee of the International Rugby Board have failed because they have never had sufficient consultation with the coaches, the players and the referees. They have failed in adding to the spectacle of the game and they must take responsibility for that. It seems that after two years of the experimental ruck and maul situation they have failed to come to a definite conclusion with regard to where they are going. This is very disappointing, for we really need to do something sooner rather than later, otherwise it will turn a lot of people away from the game at a time when money and interest in the last decade have poured into rugby. It simply should not be allowed to happen.

There is always a danger that we could turn Rugby Union into a thugs' game if we persist in making laws which encourage coaches to employ freakily big men to bash the opposition into submission. Certainly, England's tour to South Africa in 1994 or South Africa's tour to New Zealand were no places for the squeamish. I do not think the game or the players themselves are any rougher than they used to be, only bigger, although we have recently observed some pretty nasty injuries in major games. What we have to do is to look at why these injuries are happening – if you get big men charging in from 20 yards, then that is a force of circumstances provided by the laws. It will be very interesting to see how these experimental laws and variations by the Scottish Rugby Union will develop. Who knows, it might be a blueprint for the future, but at least they are trying. They will obviously base further judgement on the experimental games and they should be warmly applauded for their efforts to improve the game.

I cannot over-emphasise that laws and their interpretation

must be treated with extraordinary care, which is something that does not appear to have been done in the past. It is decent, sensible and understandable laws which will provide us with the game we want and, for the future, the administrators must look to creating a spectacle and a greater game than we have at present, because rugby in its purest form is a truly wonderful game.

Refereeing has always been another problem area and maybe we are not attracting people of sufficiently high calibre because we do not accord them the status which they deserve for doing what is probably the most thankless task of all in rugby football. Almost every Rugby Union in the world is constantly short of these officials and that tells us something. Nowadays, being a leading referee can provide as interesting a life and even more travel than is enjoyed by the players themselves. They do, of course, have to put up with a great deal of aggravation from the players and the spectators alike.

The referee is always faced with having to sort out players who are too uncompromising, downright dirty and sometimes even pathological. He has the most difficult job in the world to do, like sending off players and then finding that everybody has closed ranks against his decision, and for that reason it is very important that the referee gets the maximum support from his Union. There are a million referee jokes, like the home captain discussing the waterlogged pitch with him and saying, 'Don't call it off, our forwards like it a bit soft.' Or the prop penalised for dropping and collapsing the scrum: 'So would you, ref, if your opponent kept asking what perfume you use!' Clive Norling always tells the story of a headstone in a Welsh cemetery with the inscription, 'Here lies an honest man and a referee.' Then with a straight face he adds, 'That proves that we bury two in the same grave in Wales.'

The qualities required for a good referee are that he must know the laws, have the wisdom of Solomon, be sympathetic to the game of rugby football, have the skin of a rhinoceros, be totally impartial and without fear or favour in dealing with any player, while a sense of humour, or even two eyes, would not go amiss.

Again, the laws of rugby football are so complex that they can be a pretty forbidding and intimidating document to a young man taking up refereeing. The law book does not tell you how to give advice and even instruction to players during the course of a game, as some of our top referees are so adept at doing – that only comes with experience.

Another big bone of contention is the degree of different interpretation and emphasis that always seems to exist between the northern and southern hemisphere referees. England recently pointed out that they are only losing matches when either southern hemisphere referees or Frenchmen are involved. One can also see the lack of knowledge and the inexperience of the South African referees during England's 1994 summer tour of the Republic, which produced some unpleasant matches and extraordinarily bad refereeing. This came to a head in that infamous game in Port Elizabeth, when Jonathan Callard became the most recent in a long line of similar injuries when he had 24 stitches, some of them perilously close to his left eye, from a brutal kick seen but, astonishingly, not punished by the referee. The decision not to suspend Tim Rodber when he was sent off after he was provoked into retaliation made a nonsense of the sanctions always imposed on players in the northern hemisphere, whether or not they are in the wrong. It is surprising how rugby officials seem to close ranks on such an occasion, thus devaluing the status of referees. It was not surprising that the French, who had Phillipe Sella sent off at the same time in Canada and suspended, albeit for a derisory one match, protested at the leniency shown to Rodber, which allowed them to, again, point the finger at perfidious Albion.

What we must always remember is that rugby could never exist without referees and more should be done to encourage old players, and others, to take up what these days can be a rewarding, but sometimes thankless job. It is essential, however, that we raise the quality and calibre of referees, for too often these days results seem to depend on the whims of the official in charge. I certainly do not need reminding of the last-minute penalty given to England in the Calcutta Cup match of 1994.

CHAPTER XI

For Love or Money

BACK IN APRIL 1994 the four Home Unions announced a massive new deal with the BBC for coverage of domestic rugby. They paid £27 million for the Five Nations Championship and BSkyB paid a further £7 million for coverage of selected League and Cup matches. That amounted to an increase of over three times on the previous contract – a staggering amount of money for an amateur sport. The very fact that the media are paying these enormous sums is an indication of the growing popularity of Rugby Union Football, but there is no obvious sign of any recognition of the part that we, the amateur players, have played in making it such an attraction. Neither is there any indication that we are going to receive even a small share of this windfall, although we are the entertainers, and at the sharp end of International Rugby we are the stars of the show.

Although we are now beginning to receive some small recompense for the extraordinary amount of hard work we put into rugby, with training at club level and the International squad sessions eating into almost all our spare time during the winter months, often to the detriment of our work, social life and families, it can hardly be said that the modern International rugby player is happy with the situation, or with the exploitation of their skills and hard work by the rugby administrators world wide.

We are also completely fed up with the hypocrisy that now surrounds us, and I sometimes wish that the issue of professionalism would just disappear because there is a blatant abuse of it all over the world, and nowhere more so, in my experience, than in South Africa. There the Press and the players talk openly about the amounts players get for playing and they all have their contracts with their respective Provincial Unions. Whilst he was in the Republic with the England team in the summer of 1994, the *Daily Mail* rugby writer, Peter Jackson, who is well known for digging out information, reported that the Natal players would receive £800 a man for beating England. If it is common knowledge, then why does the International Board also not know it?

On his return from South Africa the Rugby Union President, Ian Beer, tore into the International Rugby Board and accused them of a lack of backbone, stating that at least two of the major rugby nations should have been expelled from the Board. He told of how players such as Will Carling, Brian Moore and Rob Andrew had come up to him and asked for things which the RFU could not concede because of IRB regulations. When they pointed out that other nations allowed such matters, he told them that they were cheating, which England were not disposed to do.

Surely the South African contravention of the amateur laws must have percolated into even IRB minds by now, and yet they have done nothing. In fact, they have condoned it by the haste with which they organised next year's World Cup in the Republic, at considerable commercial risk due to the uncertainties that might have followed in the wake of the new democratic elections on 27 April 1994. The Welsh Rugby Union published an official report by Vernon Pugh QC, stating that the Welsh players, and therefore presumably the other players involved, all received considerable sums of money for celebrating the South African Centenary. All the IRB keeps saying is that they cannot prove it. It seems to me that they are only a talking shop and are as inept and useless as the United Nations were in Bosnia and Rwanda. They have given everybody the impression that they have no teeth and are 'all things to all men'.

There are now many underhand payments being paid, not only in South Africa, but in Australia, New Zealand, England, Wales and Ireland. I do not mind that, but it irritates me that the only one of the senior countries where this does not happen is Scotland. I am not bitter about it, but I wish people would say what is going on and stand up and be counted against such hypocrisy, so that every rugby player in the world is performing on the same level playing field. How many International players in other countries pay an annual subscription to their club for the entitlement of being a playing member? We do in Scotland and I pay an annual subscription of £40 to Watsonians for the privilege of playing.

In Ireland there is no doubt that a number of players are now switching clubs, and presumably they are doing so for a reason. I also know that players in England and Wales are getting housing subsidies. They may not be paid for actually playing but, if the club is paying five or six hundred pounds a month for housing, that is a hell of a lot of money. It is said that the Llanelli Rugby Club have reached an agreement with their local tax office in regard to the amount that they can actually pay a player as legitimate expenses before being taxed. If you include travelling expenses, special diets and clothing etc, this can amount to a considerable sum.

All I want is for everything to come out into the open and that the usual economic laws be brought into force. In the case of supply and demand, if you are good enough and wanted enough, then there will be a market price for you, instead of all this under-hand rushing around. At the moment there is no loyalty to clubs; loyalty will only come when open transfer fees are paid and players will have to perform for the money they receive. That will be the only loyalty a player will have in the future, and the sole hold the club will have over a player is the fact that they pay him and he has a contract. Therefore, if you, as a player, want to leave a club, then at least the club will have some sort of recompense by selling on your contract. I am not really advocating all this but that is the way it will surely go. In Rugby Union it is now imperative to clear up the laws and acknowledge that players are able to openly earn money by negotiating with the club, and to earn money from off-the-field activities, even if they are 'rugby related', which at present is the clause used by the IRB to keep players away from some big money.

At the moment, everyone is looking after their own little corner and trying to secure, by whatever means, quality players to play for their club. Again, everyone knows and admits to what is going on and yet no one is doing anything about it, so why not clean up the whole awful mess?

Apart from the major English and Welsh gate-taking clubs, the only money that is washing around is at International level, because it is the countries of the Five Nations who receive these big television fees, sponsorships and vast gates. In some cases the ticket revenue and sponsorship are now over a million pounds a match. You must remember that the Provincial Unions in the southern hemisphere are similar to the Five Nations, so, again, it is at that level where the money lies. They now have a new structured competition called the Super-10 Series that enables them to have a very much higher profile in all three countries, Australia, New Zealand and South Africa, where there is a sort of cross-fertilization, not only of rugby techniques and style but of the various goings-on in the commercial world of the rugby players themselves.

The Super-10 series was a success from the start because the sponsors, the South African Broadcasting Corporation, basically underwrote the competition and used their sports channel called Topsport in the running of it in South Africa. There are other sponsors, including Qantas, who provide a significant cost-cutting exercise in regard to flying everybody to and from the various countries.

The whole structure of the game in Britain needs to be examined. The top players in England and Wales are graduating towards three or four clubs in each country, which, although it makes it easier to identify their best players, will in the end make them introverted. In Scotland, where there is no money to divert players from one club to another and where, therefore, the loyalty to a club is that much stronger, it is less insular, but then we have the problem of too great a dilution of talent and our competitive levels fail to be strong enough. I believe the English and Welsh Rugby Unions are shooting themselves in the foot because there is no cross-fertilization and their rugby will become stale. Some would argue that English rugby has already become stagnant and some of their performances during their tour in South Africa in 1994 were indicative of that. It was only their incredible performance in the first Test that prevented further criticism being made.

We have the potential to create a provincial or a top club series within the whole of the UK along the lines of the Super-10 that would be very high profile and yet would still leave a place open for the unique Five Nations Tournament.

Earlier I have given my arguments for summer rugby and I am convinced that the longer we leave it, and the opportunities for a new competitive structure, then the gap between us in Britain and the southern hemisphere countries, including Western Samoa and the other Pacific islands, will become greater and greater.

To come back to the monied clubs like Bath, Leicester, Harlequins, Cardiff, Llanelli and Swansea, that is where the majority of

International players are playing, so why not create an élite competition between such clubs and the Scottish and Irish Provinces, which could be run along similar lines to the Currie Cup in South Africa, the National Provincial Championship in New Zealand, or even the Super-10 Series? The problem with the British game is that there are too many vested interests and too much national prejudice in the four different countries and, therefore, they all tend to be ultra-conservative.

The Rugby Football Union are just rebuilding their Twickenham stadium at huge cost and they will be in hock for some time, for they are already in the red on the East Stand while starting to build the new West Stand. Both England and Scotland will have the most modern football stadia in Britain, and for Murrayfield only to be filled to capacity a few times a year is an absolute outrage. If, for instance, Leicester came up to play Edinburgh in a structured tournament, then they could draw a considerable gate of many thousands. Similarly, if the Welsh club champions such as Swansea were to play the English champions, Bath, you might fill the ground, because there is no doubt that people want to see top players playing in a top-level competition, and this could be best served by my idea of a sort of British or European Super-10.

Strangely, there is no place for provincial rugby in England because, just as in the divisional matches, they would fail to find an identity. That is why I suggest that England use their top clubs such as Bath, Harlequins, Gloucester, Leicester, Northampton and Wasps. In Wales you have got Swansea, Cardiff, Llanelli, Neath and the new kid on the block, Pontypridd. To get up to these standards, we in Scotland and Ireland would have to play our provincial sides, and it is only on that basis that you could have a national championship throughout the whole of the UK which would provoke tremendous interest from the four different nations playing in a fantastic competition. You would probably start off with five teams from England, three from Wales and two each from Ireland and Scotland in the first division, and a similar number in the second, with promotion and relegation running up and down into the respective national leagues.

These players, of course, would be semi-professional, for that is the way the game is evolving. Players who want only to play for the love of the game, and there are a tremendous number of them, will find their own level in which to play, but those who commit most of their time to playing at the highest level will be well rewarded, and I think everybody can now see the sense of that.

I have no doubt that such a structure would produce a different type of game, played by a different sort of person. That does not mean that professional and business men, doctors, dentists, lawyers and marketing executives, will have no future in Rugby Union and be excluded. It is every individual's choice as to whether they want to pursue a career or whether they want to play full-time rugby.

Everyone has that choice and if someone is still able to pursue a career in medicine while pursuing a cap, then good luck to him. However, if he cannot, he may wish to postpone his career and say, 'I want to give rugby a go for five years', and therefore he must be compensated for that. They will only have a future in rugby if they devote time to it, for that is the way the game is changing, with players becoming full-time athletes. Nowadays there is no getting away from that sort of dedication and if that means that you have to perform and train with terrific commitment to play International Rugby, you have to accept it and go with the flow, because if you do not, you will never get to the top. There will always be those who are prepared to dedicate themselves and put in the time, effort, willingness, drive and desire to get to be a Test match player, particularly if they are to be well rewarded. That, in turn, could mean even greater commitment.

In Britain, we still have an awful lot to learn about the marketing of the game, whereas in South Africa, Australia and New Zealand the game is sold superbly, especially through television. I think the Australians are probably the best marketeers and they have learned much from the slick selling of Rugby League in Australia, also through television.

In many ways that unique competition called the Five Nations Tournament is both a massive success and an albatross against change. The southern hemisphere nations have always been intensely envious of our Five Nations Championship because of the tremendous crowds and revenues that it brings in. It has been the principal driving force in northern hemisphere rugby and one that, in the past, has kept France in check, in terms of moderating their aggressive attitude in favour of professionalism. It will, therefore, always have its place as one of the great tournaments of the world but what we must do is look at the structure beneath that and build up to a crescendo for the Five Nations. I believe that if people put their national prejudice aside and looked at the wider British scene, or perhaps including France, then we could have the most magnificent structure, which would put rugby into a different sphere. It is already happening and there is no doubt that when you market the game properly it will develop an even greater following and there will be huge support for all these games. That is why the television companies are now paying £34 million, because they know that there is something big there.

Rugby is also becoming a young man's game and there will be very few players playing rugby at a high level after the age of 30 in the next few years. I am convinced that rugby players will get capped at a younger age and they will be finished by the time they are in their late twenties because of the growing physical nature of the sport. You will only be able to play so many years of International Rugby and whether you start at 20 or 24 that limit will be about seven or eight years.

Every leading rugby player that I meet around the world is now in agreement that the game will soon be entirely professional at the highest level, and it strikes me that the sooner it happens the better for everyone. We will have to learn from the experiences of soccer and the way athletics has gone, and there is no point in pretending that it will be an easy route.

The big money in athletics goes largely only to the very top athletes who skim off the lion's share and perhaps rugby administrators can learn from that and ensure that the spread is more even. This is essential in a game like rugby, where a prop forward or a lock is generally of a lower profile than, say, a fly half. Sometimes professionalism can get out of control, as it seems to have done in tennis where player power very often takes over and the top people skim off the cream, leaving very little for the others. It is no wonder that tennis suddenly began to ail as an international sport as the players became too big for their tennis shoes.

In a team sport such as rugby, player power is all very well, but first the individual has to be selected for his country. If they are not selected because they are not good enough, then suddenly their market value will drop dramatically. It is also self-evident that they are dependent on the players around them, like the way those, sometimes anonymous, forwards give them the ball to play with. You can see, therefore, why, in rugby football, I would prefer to see a wider distribution of any monies accruing going to the team as a whole. Team players are very much at the whim of the selectors and they have to keep on performing to a very high standard if they are to keep their place in a national side. If all they are doing is rushing around trying to make as much money as possible from commercial interests, then their rugby will ultimately suffer and, if it falls off, they are not going to get selected.

You may argue that all these players who migrate from South Africa, Australia and New Zealand to countries like Italy and, to a lesser extent, France during their close seasons at home, are not only mercenaries, because they are certainly not doing it for love of the game but for money, but they are also not doing their game much good because, by playing rugby for 12 months of the year, there is no time to rest and they become stale. Obviously these players are making hay while the sun shines and, even if their rugby is suffering as a result, they know that they are being well compensated. There can be no doubt that selectors for national sides want their players to be fresh and fit for the Test matches and, some time in the future, they will not be prepared to play tired players. When that time comes, perhaps the players will be compensated in other ways.

Often, when teams become successful, the players get above themselves and make demands, which currently their individual Rugby Unions are unable to concede. The English players, for instance, appear to be in a constant confrontational position with the RFU, whereas the Scottish players are much more in tune with their Union. The England players have tended to go along a particular track, without explanation to the relevant Union committee, and then have tried to justify their actions afterwards. In Scotland, the players have been more patient and we have found that the Union has come around to our way of thinking. It has not happened overnight, but over a period of three or four years. I now think they are fairly supportive and that is the only way we can go forward.

It strikes me that the Unions in the southern hemisphere are also very pro their players over rewards for selection to the national squad, and the only Union that appears out of step with their players is the RFU, simply because of the confrontational way that the England players have tried to force their hand. I do not believe that has worked to the players' benefit. The England players have been successful on the field and there are enough Pressmen and supporters clamouring on their behalf; but although they have had more people trying to force the issue, there are not many happy committee men on the current RFU who are one hundred per cent behind what the England players have done. People say, 'But then the England players have achieved greater financial rewards than we have in Scotland because of their militancy.' That may or may not be true, but they have been a far more successful side than Scotland over a longer period, they have a much larger marketplace and they receive more widespread publicity and exposure than we do. I am not in any way envious of them; all I am saying is that we have the full support of our Union, whereas the English team do not appear to have widespread support from the RFU.

An illustration of this was supplied by Stephen Jones, the well-respected rugby correspondent of the *Sunday Times*, when he wrote an article in his paper on 12 June 1994 (the day after England had lost the second Test), concerning the sending off of Tim Rodber in that evil game against Eastern Province, for which Rodber received no suspension. Jones said, 'The relationship between the team and the RFU hierarchy has been so frigid on this tour, that if Rodber had indeed been banned on Ian Beer's presidential decree, I am convinced that the team would have threatened to refuse to have played the Test.'

Within Scotland's smaller market there is still a big demand for players to make personal appearances and speaking engagements, or whatever commercial public relations a company requires. Therefore the players are doing reasonably well out of it, but if you think that is what drives a player forward I urge you to think again. What the Scottish team wants, and has always wanted above all else, is victory on the field of play and no one is more disappointed than I am when we fail to achieve that success. You are not going to get too many companies or sponsors queuing up to support you as a team or as an individual if you are not flourishing, so first and foremost the Scottish rugby team, or any other side, must be as successful as they possibly can. Sponsors only want to be part of that prosperity and it simply will not work any other way.

I am always asked to quantify what I have had out of the game of rugby football in financial terms, but that is between me and the taxman. However, I have a fairly high profile within the game and, again, I stress this is because of the tremendously hard work that I have put in over the years, which makes me a marketable commodity, with business people prepared to use me to promote products or endorse their services. I am comfortable with that situation and I would be pretty silly if I did not take advantage of such a scenario. After all the hard work and the tremendous sacrifices that I have made for my rugby career, I do not think that one person in the world would begrudge me any of the compensation and commercial payback which I can command, even if it has been rugby-related because of my persona on the field of play. Nevertheless, you still have to deliver something tangible for a fee, and often that means going along and being polite to five hundred people during a lunchtime or of an evening, and travelling many hours from your home and back. You actually have to give them something that they want, so I work very hard at that and try to make sure that these sponsors get value for money.

As far as the Scottish team as an entity is concerned, I repeat, we have worked hard to get alongside our Union and we accepted that the Union's lawyers and our own appointed lawyers drew up a Players Trust Fund agreement. We achieved that in the summer of 1992 but it took a good few months and when the whole matter was put into operation we were all reasonably happy with the finished product. We employed Ian McLauchlan to be the players' agent and he has handled all affairs on behalf of the players and continues to do so. There have been a number of teething problems to overcome, but basically there is a structure in place that allows the players to go out and do personal appearances on a commercial basis, with the full approval of the Scottish Rugby Union, with all money going into the team fund.

The only grievance that I have is that the incentives and the opportunities open to the players are much greater elsewhere than in Scotland because, as a rugby nation, we tend to be out on a limb in the club and provincial sense and therefore the only way we can get into the bigger time, outside International rugby, is for the British administrators generally to put their national prejudice aside and create that all-Britain or European competitive structure that I advocate earlier in this chapter. In Scotland we recognise we have to make the most of the structure that we have, but it is only at the national level that we are able to give companies like the Royal Bank of Scotland, the Famous Grouse and all those other people who support Scottish rugby players, real value for money; for, at least, we command a lot of media attention in the Five Nations Tournament.

All these companies like to be associated with a good, clean-cut image and Scottish rugby has always possessed this characteristic. For our size and the resources available to us, a fair amount of success has been achieved in the last ten years; it eluded us in 1994, but out of our failure we might well see the real qualities of the Scots coming to the fore. It will make everyone more determined to work hard, to try and seek greater success during World Cup year, which is very important to the Scottish psyche. It is hoped

Watsonians on tour in Aspen, Colorado, 1992

Another photocall, Murrayfield, 1994 (photograph: Daily Record)

Hey Will, who's going to be captain of the Lions? Twickenham, 1993 (photograph: Daily Record)

British Isles Rugby Union team to New Zealand, 1993

Scoring the winning try against the New Zealand Maoris in Wellington
(photograph: Daily Record*)*

Second Test victory against the All Blacks in Wellington: (top) Ieuan Evans in action with myself and Scott Gibbs in close support; (bottom) the smiles say it all. With Geech in the tunnel

With Diane in 1993: my Lioness at Edinburgh Airport welcoming me home from the Lions Tour (photograph: Hamish Campbell)

The best day of my life – the only perfect match I've ever had! (photograph: Daily Record)

Mike Hall closing in on a big catch, Cardiff, 1994

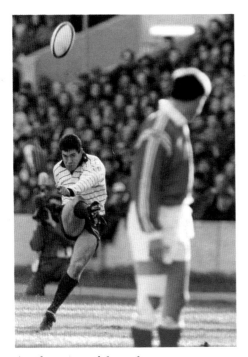

*Another successful penalty
(photograph:* Daily Record)

*Some liquid refreshment prior to goal-
kicking practice (photograph:* Daily
Record)

Rob Wainwright scoring the only try of the game, Murrayfield, 1994 (photograph: Daily Record*)*

With Gary holding my balls, I couldn't miss! (photograph: Daily Record*)*

Golf – my other true love, Dalmahoy, 1994 (photograph: Fotosport)

that the blooding of new young players during Scotland's tour to Argentina in the summer of 1994 will develop and throw up new players.

The World Cup in South Africa in 1995 will inevitably give a huge further stimulus to converting the game from amateur to professional. South Africa will be a wonderful country to host the World Cup, with its magnificent stadia and playing surfaces. It is a fabulous country for rugby supporters to visit, not only because white South Africans, and many of its black and coloured population, are passionate about their rugby, but because it is a land of great beauty and contrasts, such as the temperate Cape in Western Province, the sub-tropical humidity of Natal, the aridity of the Kalahari, and the equatorial ambience of the Kruger Park in North East Transvaal. As long as the new government are prepared to guarantee the safety not only of the players but of the many supporters, then the World Cup in South Africa could be one of the most enjoyable experiences that any rugby lover could have.

Certainly, the post-election actions of Nelson Mandela in rebuilding national unity have astonished and delighted the whole world. The omens are therefore looking good, not only for the political and economic future of South Africa, but also for the rugby community, who can now look forward to a memorable World Cup. What a shame that apartheid should have divided a nation for so long and that the resultant boycotts kept South Africa out of world sport for almost three decades! They are, as England found to their cost during the summer of 1994, one of the mightiest rugby nations of all, and even the awesome All Blacks have had to be second best. The statistics are there to prove it, for New Zealand have never won a Test series in the Republic, even though they beat them in a one-off game in 1992.

The reason why I say that the World Cup will provoke a further advance to flat-out professionalism is because Dr Louis Luyt, who has taken over from the legendary Dr Danie Craven as rugby supremo in that country and who promises to be every bit as controversial as Danie, is a devout believer that players who have to train and perform to professional standards, with ever increasing media coverage and the attendant implications of the tremendous pressures thus produced, should be treated not like amateurs but as paid professionals.

In June 1994, during England's tour of South Africa, Ian Beer, the Rugby Union Football President, lectured the 22 Provincial Rugby Union presidents and the South African Rugby Board that

South Africa were wrongly taking the road to professionalism. The sharp response of Louis Luyt, President of the South African Rugby Football Union, was, 'You don't believe in professionalism. You are a pure amateur. I believe in amateurism, but I am a true professional.'

There is no evidence that a professional Rugby Union game, which can only exist at the more senior levels of the game, will alter the nature of the game in any way. After all, many players throughout the world are already receiving remuneration for playing and it does not seem to have affected people, like David Campese, who have been playing professional rugby for years. He is still one of the game's most vivacious and skilful entertainers and is quite a character off the field, even if he does tend to be his own man. Rugby is no different from any other sport; it needs its champions, its heroes and its entertainers. If you were to wipe out all those, then the support and, ultimately, the game itself would be dead.

Rugby involves people from all walks of life, from different backgrounds, in a multitude of different countries. If you happen to be one of those who is good enough to get paid, then it does not stop the other guys going out on a Saturday afternoon and enjoying themselves in much the same way as millions of soccer players around the world have a kick around on a Sunday afternoon or play for pub teams; or golfers who, week in, week out, play golf without begrudging the likes of Nick Faldo, Greg Norman or Fred Couples their fame or their fortune.

In many cases what we have these days is an ancient set of administrators who do not see eye to eye with the younger people in the game. They are all protecting their own territories and, quite honestly, they have had a marvellous life over the years, with great opportunities for travel and for hosting various people from all over the world. We must not forget, however, that most of them work extremely hard for their position and make valuable contributions to the various organisations and Unions which they represent. It is surely time that, as the game becomes professional, then professional people should be employed to administer it.

The days of the part-timer and the amateur committee man are over, because they simply do not have the time or the necessary expertise to devote to a fast-changing scene. Already the four Home Unions have fallen well behind in the marketing of the game in the United Kingdom and serious consideration must now be given to the handing over of the administration to professional people who will promote and market rugby. Knowing the commercial values of everything that is involved, from ground advertising to television, and all the attendant marketing, is a full-time job and anyone on any of the Unions who doubts that should not be involved in the game. You simply cannot have these massive sums of money, such as the millions coming in from television over the next three years, together with huge gate monies and sponsorships, and not have professional people handling that money.

I come back to the truism that the best way to market any game is through its top players selling the sport to the public by their skills and efforts on the field. It is, therefore, totally mad and archaic to say that rugby players are not allowed to be seen advertising in rugby kit unless it is for a team or Union sponsor. What difference does it make whether a player advertises in rugby kit and boots? He is merely using the persona and charisma he has achieved in the game to help promote a product. You cannot tell me that Will Carling or Ieuan Evans are known as Will Carling the businessman or Ieuan Evans the businessman. They have earned their reputation and name by their performances on the rugby field, which have placed them in demand as a marketing tool, and they are entitled to exploit that. There should not be any archaic rules telling players what they cannot wear to promote themselves and their sport, and that should be the end of it.

Having lived on the cusp of the change from amateur to professional, I am probably a victim of my own ambiguity. I think that each International team and Union should set up a trust fund for the players, from which they could collect some years after they retire. If you have played 50 times for your country, then perhaps you would get some £25,000 plus the accrued interest, and if you played 30 times then proportionately you would be paid £15,000 or whatever, but it would be related to the number of times you had represented your country. They could, of course, receive some of it immediately, to help with education or setting up home, but I would like the bulk of it given in a lump sum or in a pension 20 years after they have finished playing, without worrying about paying players on a match to match basis, because a lot of them would simply go out and spend it instead of investing it for the future. Why not just invest the money earned in a trust fund, actively manage the fund and distribute it to the player, say at the age of 50? In that way we could still ensure that rugby footballers play the game in the context of a fairly normal working life, and perhaps satisfy both the amateur ethic and those who want to drive the game into flat-out professionalism.

CHAPTER XII

The Alternative Rugby Life

I HAVE TALKED mainly about the big time. There is, however, a far bigger and more real world in the lower levels of rugby football, where I am convinced there is more fun, if only by virtue of possessing a totally different sense of values. There rugby is played largely as a pastime, with no great pressures concerning the outcome. Nevertheless, no matter what level of rugby you play, it remains that what stands out is the enjoyment you get from winning games and socialising in the bar afterwards.

Touring is one of those activities which can give you enormous pleasure, whether you are only going down the road 20 miles with your local club or if you are off with an International team to the other side of the world. The memories brought back from each of these tours remain with you for the rest of your life, even if they concern only the extramural activities when the scores are long forgotten. It is all about having communion and fun with friends with whom you play rugby, week in and week out, and you are always able to recall and retail the joy and sometimes the difficult moments, which in turn become amusing, and often apocryphal, in the telling.

Of my many fun trips overseas, the one that stands out more than any other is the Hong Kong Sevens, which I have been lucky enough to attend on four or five occasions. I have also been on rugby tours to Singapore, Amsterdam and Lisbon, and spent time out in Vail and Aspen in Colorado. The common denominator on all those occasions was the friendships, the people that I met and, as the Irish say, 'the crack' that I enjoyed, both on and off the field.

The first time I went to Hong Kong was the week after we won the Grand Slam against England in 1990. I went with my brother Scott, Iwan Tukalo and Derek Turnbull, and the first pleasurable thing that happened to us was that we were upgraded on the Cathay Pacific flight. As it was shortly after our great triumph and we were still celebrating, when we stopped at Dubai on the way out we were pretty happy guys and did not know what state of play we were at. I had bought a video camcorder about a month previously and I had used it a sufficient number of times to be able to understand all the controls. However, looking back, the results of my filming in the toyshop of the Dubai duty free were an absolute scream and said much about the state we were in. Back on the plane, we demolished a few more G & Ts and a few more bottles of champagne before arriving at Hong Kong, which is the most spectacular arrival of any airport in the world, for when you are doing a right turn coming into land, you are passing blocks of flats so close that you can actually see the television in people's living-rooms or women doing their ironing, which is really quite extraordinary, as David Coleman might say.

We arrived in Hong Kong not knowing what to expect and, when we left five days later, we were dying to get home, for our bodies could not cope with any more alcohol, which the extraordinary number of Scottish people out there insisted on pouring into us to celebrate the Grand Slam. We were playing in the Hong Kong Tens, a ten-a-side tournament held on the Wednesday and Thursday prior to the weekend Sevens, and we had arranged to stay with a fine guy called Jimmy Gibson, who had married a local girl. He had been working as an architect out there for 20 years and he very kindly put the four of us up. I am not sure that he told his wife because when we arrived later that morning she seemed a wee bit upset and worried about the trouble that we might bring. I will always remember the Saturday night between the two days of the Sevens, and desperately needing an early night following two nights when I was out until six or seven in the morning. Arriving back early at Jimmy's house, I put on the air conditioning because it was so hot and humid. Unfortunately, there was no light in the bedroom and I was just lying there, twisting and turning and sweating like a pig, with the air conditioning not seeming to help. When morning came I was swimming in perspiration, not having had any sleep whatsoever, and discovered that I had switched the air conditioning unit to hot instead of cold! I decided the best way to get through Sunday was to drink continuously and so we did not see much of the Sevens during the day but, when we got back to the UK, I again saw the evidence on my video camera of our prolonged celebration – the camera angles were awry, to say the least.

I returned the following year to play for a northern hemisphere side against the southern hemisphere. When I accepted the invitation, I did not realise that we would play against a full ANZAC team in which David Campese was playing at full back, with John Kirwan and Ian Williams on the wings. There was Michael Hawker at centre, together with Joe Stanley, Grant Fox and Nick Farr-Jones. Then there was John Drake, Steve McDowell, Sean Fitzpatrick, Gary Whetton and Steve Cutler, and the back row was Simon Poidevin, Jeff Miller and Zinzan Brooke. Needless to say, the northern hemisphere side was nowhere near as powerful, although we had Jason Leonard and Mike Teague of the England Grand Slam side of 1991. It was extremely tough and difficult, and although we played out of our skins we still lost by about 30 points, but fortunately it teemed with tropical rain and the score was not as large as it might have been. We were lucky!

I suffered from dehydration and instead of attending the sponsor's dinner after the game I ended up in bed at 8 p.m. and slept for about 15 hours. I was just catching up on sleep, something that all rugby tourists will understand and know about, for you simply do not consider sleep when you are on a rugby tour, nor do you bother much about eating. I remember a saying that I once heard, 'Eating's cheating, food is for kids.' I have often reminded myself of that when I have been starving on tour, for touring stories are all about drinking, not eating.

On my third visit to Hong Kong in 1992 I captained the Barbarians in the Sevens. Unfortunately, we had a couple of withdrawals. Derek Stark, who was to be our speed man, got injured the weekend before we were due to leave but because a replacement could not be found he came anyway. We were also promised a coach, but Dick Best could not turn up until a couple of days before the tournament. In the event we did not do very well and we fell to South Korea in the quarter finals. Nevertheless, Hong Kong is special and is probably the most exotic and most exciting location of any rugby event in the world. It is one vast bar and playground for rugby people from all over the world and it is an absolutely fantastic experience.

There is always a post-tournament dinner, which is quite

amazing, with all the participating teams putting on their own ethnic cabaret turn. I remember one year that my brother Scott was attending the dinner in the Hong Kong Hilton and was chatting with Wayne Smith, that superlative All Black stand off, who is also a very fine exponent of Sevens, and Scott said to Wayne, 'I'll race you over to the other side of the room.' 'Right, you're on, no problem,' said Wayne, but Scott made a condition that their feet were not to touch the ground. Inevitably, the tables started to collapse as they jumped between them, like stepping stones crossing a river, and by the time they had reached the other side of the room they had left a trail of firewood. Most hotel managers would have taken a pretty dim view and said that enough was enough, and there was no way that they would have the Sevens dinner there the following year. However, another Scotsman by the name of James Smith, who is the great general manager of the Hong Kong Hilton and a truly wonderful guy, merely took the decision that if they were going to have the dinner the next year, which they did, then they would make sure that the tables were strong enough to hold the likes of Scott and Wayne. That sort of indulgence appears to be the attitude in Hong Kong when the Sevens are on. You could say that it is a rugby player's paradise.

There are many famous bars in Hong Kong and none more famous than Joe Bananas down in Wanchai. It remains open 24 hours a day throughout the week of the Sevens, and the queues still stretch 50 yards long at five in the morning. It seems that people flock from all corners of the world to get into Joe Bananas and, unfortunately, when you go on tour with Jason Leonard, you are simply not allowed to leave before they start serving breakfast at seven in the morning. Only then are you allowed to go back to the hotel and grab a few hours sleep. I went with Jason again in 1994 to play in the Hong Kong Tens for the Quality Street Gang. Jason is a tremendous ambassador for English rugby because he is just one hell of a guy and a bloody marvellous tourist. Jason would have a drink between rounds, but it still did not put him off playing a typically hard and entertaining game of rugby. He used to delight in getting out on the wing and charging down the touchline for people to bounce off him as they came into the tackle. Jason is one of those genuine rugby characters and it is a shame there are not more people like him playing International rugby. I had the great pleasure of rooming with him and occasionally he would be my alarm call, as he came to bed every morning at eight o'clock – just as I was getting up.

Another terrific touring location in the Far East is Singapore, where lucky teams get to play in the Singapore Cricket Club Sevens. We managed to convince a number of the senior partners in Richard Ellis, the chartered surveyors with whom I was working at the time, that it would be a very good piece of public relations to take a team to Singapore. The local office were already involved in sponsoring the tournament and, at the time, Michael Lynagh was working with Richard Ellis in Australia. Other members of the team were Andrew Harriman, who is one of the greatest Sevens exponents of all time; Richard Cramb, a Scottish cap at outside half; Mark Thomas, who subsequently played for Wales in the Rugby World Cup Sevens in 1993; together with some good soldiers such as John Ellison, Nick Barnes-Batty and Geoff Ellis. We were ably led by Philip Dawe and Andrew Yeandle, the ex-Cardiff wing, who was another marvellous guy to go on tour with. We tried to convince Richard Ellis that we would have to fly out business class, but failed on account of cost. Nevertheless, we were togged out with lovely blazers, trousers, shirts and ties.

We went to Singapore two years running, but I had damaged my groin the first year and as a result was unable to play in the tournament. I made up for that by keeping the team supplied with copious amounts of Singapore Slings between rounds, as well as organising all the social activities, which included water skiing, visits to bars and various other relaxation activities.

I remember Andrew Yeandle had a rubber chicken, which was our tour mascot, and for some strange reason the Singaporeans went absolutely potty when they caught sight of it. One year I was in charge of it temporarily and, unfortunately, I left it in the back of a taxi when we were going to a beautiful seafood restaurant. This was inexcusable and I got absolute hell from Yeandle. I was totally distraught and I phoned the taxi cab company, but to no avail, for although they chased around, they failed to find the chicken. We proceeded to make a big thing of this and convened a Press conference. A couple of days later, in the Sunday papers, there was a full page article and a cartoon of me chasing after this dreadful rubber chicken. As a penance, I was forced by the rest of the team to go around with a bright red wig in the boiling 85 degrees temperature and high humidity. It was uncomfortable and embarrassing to say the least.

It was during the after-match party at the Singapore Sevens that I came across the most incredible party piece I have ever seen in my life. The Sun Solarians, a team of big drinkers from The Sun

Inn, Richmond, were out there and one of their chaps drank six pints of milk; first two ordinary and normal coloured milks, then he had two chocolate-flavoured milks, and finally two strawberry-flavoured. Then he asked which coloured milk we would like to see. We shouted back, 'Strawberry', so he promptly regurgitated a pint of strawberry milk. 'Which colour next?' he would ask and we would shout, 'Chocolate'. He would duly deliver a pint of chocolate-coloured milk, followed finally by a pint of white milk.

It was an incredible sight, and the only people that did not seem to enjoy it were the New Zealand team from Ponsonby, who arrived two hours after the party started and left an hour before it finished. This typical sobriety and non-socialising of the New Zealand teams, even when on a fun tour, still baffles me. I can never quite understand why they are not able to relax in the same way as other teams from around the world.

I also remember the little Japanese chap, who must only have been about 18, yet he could drink a half pint of beer quicker than anyone I ever saw, and we decided that we would try and see if we could beat him. Twenty of us lined up, one behind the other, all with our half pints of beer, and, despite our being pretty big lads, we never came close to beating him. Even though he was collapsing between half pints, his team-mates would prop him up, slap him about the face and he would carry on to comprehensively beat the rest of us. It was an astonishing sight.

Touring is far more enjoyable when you play rugby in hot countries, and I think that is why I have advocated so strongly the playing of rugby in the summer in the United Kingdom. Obviously, everyone appreciates not having to put on track suits and wear training tops between ties during Sevens competitions, or prior to warming up for a game. The beauty about all these exotic tours, to Hong Kong, Singapore, Lisbon and Amsterdam, is that generally they take place in lovely weather and therefore you enjoy yourself so much more. I believe that Britain could organise the same sort of tournaments with a party atmosphere during the summer when, let us face it, everyone could relish it so much more if they were not freezing their butts off, or being forced to watch a tournament in terrible conditions.

One year we went to Monte Carlo to play in the Glenlivet Monte Carlo Sevens in the Prince Rainier Stadium and it was absolutely superb. The only problem was that the French did not support it sufficiently and there were more players taking part in the competition than there were spectators. One of the beauties of the tournament was that it was only played over one afternoon and evening, from about three o'clock on the Sunday, which left you free to appreciate the rest of the weekend on the beach amongst some lovely, attractive ladies, and at night out enjoying the sights and entertainments of Monte Carlo. The highlight of the weekend was the official banquet in the remarkable Empire Grand Ballroom in the Hotel de Paris, with Prince Albert as the guest of honour. They had the most wonderful trumpeters from the Marines Band, whose party trick was to go up behind the ladies going to the loos, poking them with their trombones and blowing fanfares.

The Scots team I was with were the Co-optimists, and we were striding along the beautiful avenue on the way to the Hotel de Paris wearing our kilts and all dressed up in our Highland dress, feeling like a million dollars, or the man who broke the bank at Monte Carlo. The kilt was a great advantage, for I remember dancing with some grand ladies who, for reasons of their own, only wanted to dance with the men in the kilts. The downside of it was that they refused to let us in the famous Casino because they said we were dressed in skirts, which was both infuriating and a great disappointment.

On the Saturday evening, in a pub, we met an East End kid made good. He had an absolutely magnificent 120-foot yacht in the harbour in Monte Carlo, and we invited him along to the rugby the next day, which he enjoyed so much that he invited us all to a party on his boat later that evening. After the official function, we trooped down to the harbour. My abiding memory of the occasion was of Mickey Skinner and Co shouting out orders for drinks and the waiter rushing off to make Pina Coladas for everybody. It was also the only time in my life that I have sipped Dom Perignon champagne. The host was so hospitable and friendly, and enjoyed himself so much at the Sevens and with us that evening, that I think we gained a convert to rugby. I could not believe that, when I returned to Monte Carlo some six years later, the guy who had been pouring drinks all night came up to me in the Texan restaurant to recount all the stories of that time.

As with every tour, I remember all those off-the-field occasions, which are usually impromptu. The memories, together with the photographs and various souvenirs, will be treasured for the rest of my life.

I had a summer in Vail, Colorado, in 1986 with my old Cambridge pals, Mark Thomas and Kelvin Wyles. We arrived at Denver after a long flight from London and we were picked up by a guy called Pat MacDonald, later to become known to us as 'Farmer', for the obvious reason. As we collected our luggage, I heard a voice saying, 'You big bastard', and I thought, 'Oh my God, who the hell knows me in this part of the world?' I turned around and realised it was a chap called Graham Waddell, the brother of one of my pals from my college days in Paisley, who had also gone out there for the summer. So it really is a small world these days.

We were there for about three months and the first training session was at about 8,500 feet above sea level, which takes some getting used to. We used to frequent a bar that was used as our unofficial club house by the rugby community and it was where we all made contact with each other after work. I remember, on my first night, getting into the spirit of things as everyone was very friendly and buying me drinks. Unfortunately, for the first time in my life I tasted upside-down Margueritas, which over-turned my world that night. I woke up with the most horrific hangover the next day and that was my introduction to the Vail Rugby Club and a splendid bunch of guys.

We used to go away on trips to rugby tournaments at all the ski towns in Colorado, such as Breckenridge, Craig, Steamboat and Aspen, who all participate in a superbly organised league. It is very small scale and very amateurish rugby, but it is all about a bunch of young guys going away for the weekend to have a great time. When you come over from the United Kingdom, you are the visiting fireman, dying to enjoy yourself in a new environment, and wanting to get away and see as much of the country as possible. I really enjoyed America and my time in Vail.

One night we were doing a round of all the bars and drinking shots of Tequila Slammers and everything else, so that we got a bit carried away. My pal, Mark Thomas, and I were walking home through Vail and we passed one of those little popcorn wagons that was parked in the town centre. Stupidly, I gave it a good old Glasgow kiss, which is a head butt, and to my horror the window just shattered in front of me. I was so stunned that it had broken that I started to laugh, and I slumped down beside the popcorn wagon. Mark Thomas said, 'Come on, you'd better run and get away from here. The cops will be here in a flash.' I was laughing so much that I simply could not move when, all of a sudden and bang on cue, the police arrived. Fortunately, Mark knew the officer and said, 'Look, just don't worry. He was a bit drunk and he tripped up and the thing got smashed, but we'll make sure it's repaired tomorrow.' The police officer took it on trust that his word was good, for Mark was actually working as a bouncer in one of the local nightclubs. I think the real reason he worked at that job was to see the girls coming in, so that he could date them and later meet up with them. In any event, he got on pretty well with the local police.

The next morning I went down to Denver for four days, without doing anything about the popcorn wagon. I phoned my flat-mate, big Scott Halstead, whom we called 'Beef', a lovely guy who looked after me very well, and said, 'Hey, Beef, what's happening?' He answered in his casual American drawl, 'Hey, when are you coming back into town?' I replied, 'I don't know, a couple of days time I guess', and he said, 'I suggest you don't.' 'Why not?' 'Because there's a warrant out for your arrest.' I thought, 'My godfathers, here we go! I'm not going to be allowed to get back home and go on tour with Cambridge University.' However, I returned to Vail and paid the popcorn wagon owner a hundred dollars and my name was cleared from the warrant. I was a little more careful from there on – and gave popcorn wagons a wide berth.

What I really enjoyed about Vail was that it was such an outdoor life. People there are used to being out of doors and they go away for the weekend, camping, climbing and fishing. One of the nice things we did was four-wheel driving, where you got a short wheel-based vehicle in four-wheel drive and drove up the dried riverbeds. We got up to about 11,000 feet and bivouacked for the night. We then climbed another couple of thousand feet on foot to the top of the mountain, where the views were absolutely stunning. I have wonderful memories of running down the mountain late at night in shorts and tee shirt, back to our camp before it became too dark. The only way we could manage it was by targeting our campfire, which had been lit by the people who had stayed behind.

I remember sitting around the campfire, telling stories and singing songs, drinking Tequila and Peach Schnapps, as well as a few beers, and feeling nostalgic for my former days in the Boy Scouts. I know I keep repeating this, but young men should always take such wonderful opportunities, to go up into the mountains like the American Rockies with their breathtaking scenery. You should take advantage of travelling to various parts of the world, to meet and live with the locals. It is only by meeting with the natives, in the broader sense of the word, that you can get the flavour of their country and enjoy the hospitality, culture and freely given friendship which is a hallmark of the Americans. My sojourn in Vail was a jewel that will remain in my mind's eye for a very long time.

On another occasion we went up to Craig for a typical ski town rugby tournament, where we all booked into the Holiday Inn. It was Saturday night and we were playing our arch-rivals, Aspen, in the final of the tournament the next day. Meanwhile all the teams were enjoying a massive party in an old corrugated iron shed. I think it was an old railway shed which was used in the wintertime as an indoor tournament venue for curling. The Vail players, who were more high-spirited than the Aspen boys, worked out a plan to bolt the two massive doors at either end and hit the main light switch at the same time, while 20 of the players outside rained stones and mini-boulders on to the roof. The noise inside must have been absolutely deafening and pretty frightening. After about ten minutes, we decided to get the hell out of there, as eventually some of those trapped were managing to get out and were desperate to see who the perpetrators were. We got away in the nick of time. Unfortunately, our lack of sleep that night contributed to a hefty drubbing from the Aspen team the following day, so we got our come-uppance. We arrived back in Vail on Sunday night, completely wrecked after a wonderful weekend, but not on the most friendly terms with the Aspen players who were still furious about the night before.

Aspen were the first team in the Rockies to have purchased a scrummaging machine, so one night the Vail boys went over to acquire it and take it back to Vail, and it was not until the boys from Aspen came over to play in Vail a couple of months later that they found their scrummaging machine, which was their pride and joy.

Rugby in America still has a large curiosity value, for people are so used to seeing American footballers wearing their big pads and helmets, almost a full suit of armour, that they simply do not understand why the rugby players indulge in such a physical game without protection. Nevertheless there is growing interest and, without question, the best tournament that I ever played in, in the States, was the Aspen Ruggerfest. Watsonians went there as part of their tour of Colorado, and were expected to do well in one of the top rugby competitions in the whole of the USA. Alas the boys succumbed to the temptations of life in the local bars and simply were unable to perform. Eight o'clock in the morning is a bit early to play matches and, unfortunately, some of our boys were just coming back from the bars when it was kick-off time – they were really not at their best. In typically hospitable fashion, the Americans wanted to reward us for having come all that way, so they voted us as the 'Best and Fairest Team', which was a very nice gesture.

This tournament attracts about five thousand people every year, and, if there is no football game on that weekend, all the girls come up from Colorado University to join in the fun. We arrived at Denver and stayed at a place called the Landmark Hotel, right across the road from Shotgun Willie's, a dancing bar. It was just the ideal venue to start a tour, and this den of iniquity was a very interesting place which certainly occupied much of the boys' attention at the start of the tour. Suffice to say we had a hell of a lot of fun.

Like most young men, and contrary to what other people think about me, I do have my dark side, and I am always slightly wary of both my own Jekyll and Hyde characteristics and those of other players on tour. One year I played with the Bahrain Warblers, who are a great fun, social side composed of hugely entertaining personalities. We were at the Lisbon Sevens and, I must admit, we went a bit too far off the rails. Eric Rush and Lindsay Raki had come over from New Zealand, and we had Mark Thomas, Iwan Tukalo and one or two others. We won the tournament and celebrated too heavily, and yours truly got a bit carried away on the port and the Baileys. I got back to the hotel rather late and Iwan had already crashed out and could not be awakened, no matter how hard I hammered on the door.

Unfortunately, in those situations my alter ego, which I call my twin brother Andrew, comes out. It was Andrew who was out to play that night and he decided that he was desperate to get to his bed, so he charged the door and the whole thing, including the door frame, completely collapsed. When Iwan had recovered from the shock, he just burst out laughing and went mental and said, 'What the hell have you done?' I do not remember too much about it but retribution soon followed, with a shock to the system when the organiser of the Lisbon Sevens, Manuel Cabrale, rang me up and said, 'Mr Hastings, we have a very serious charge against you, and you are going to have to pay the bill for some three hundred pounds.' Fortunately I managed to knock that down to about two hundred, and I am glad that Andrew has not surfaced on too many occasions. He is an expensive chap to go on tour with and certainly he is not the nicest of persons, tending to go off the rails when he has had too many drinks.

Another time with the Warblers, we were in Stockholm for a ten-a-side festival and it was my stag weekend. It was an interesting place to go for a four-day stag party and my best man, Dave 'Spam' Buchanan, was with us, my pal Mark Thomas and other luminaries such as Damian Cronin, Sean Lineen, Pete Taylor, Everton Davies, Colin Hillman and my brother Scott. We were kept a bit in line by the fact that we were playing two days of rugby, but we really had a terrific time. We went to a place called Café Opera, which must be one of the most fabulous nightclubs I have ever been to in my life. There were about 22 of us and we ate and drank magnificently, and heavily. When the bill came at the end of the evening it was fifteen hundred pounds, which Chris Neill, a top man from down South, paid for with his American Express Chargecard. Well done, Chris! I think we still owe you a couple of beers for that.

The following night, after we had won the Stockholm Tens trophy, we were again into big-time celebrating at the Café Opera, with champagne and everything else going into the trophy. I was not feeling all that well and could not face the thought of a drink, so I went for a walk with Scott and Colin Hillman but, when we came back about an hour and a half later, Mr Tukalo, to show his displeasure at my departure, filled the cup up with champagne, beer, tomato juice and everything else they had drunk during my absence, and made me drink the whole thing down as a punishment for leaving the party. He also ordered me 14 Slippery Nipples, which I hasten to add is a cocktail of Baileys and Sambucca, but luckily he was so drunk that, when the waiter arrived, he banged into him and the Slippery Nipples went mostly over himself. I ended up only having to drink four – which probably saved my life.

Not surprisingly, another horrendous bill, this time for sixteen hundred pounds, arrived and then Simon Davies, who, with Henry Peevers, is the founder and organiser of the Bahrain Warblers, one of the world's most popular touring sides, volunteered to pay. So, Chris and Simon, we really were very appreciative and my stag weekend was a wonderful experience – but not one that I would wish to repeat, for I was fortunate to survive it.

My abiding memory of that weekend was not only the size of the bills for some magnificent parties, but how the human body can take so much punishment and so little sleep. The party on the last night continued in the hotel jacuzzi until half past five in the morning, when finally I went upstairs to change and go off to the airport. I arrived in the office in London that morning, did a couple of hours work and then, I am afraid, I had to leave and catch the flight home to Scotland and crash out for the next two days. I am lucky to have such understanding employers and to have survived it all. Touring is now in my blood, so it will come as no surprise to you that my honeymoon, with my lovely wife Diane, took place in the Far East and was simply wonderful.

Chapter XIII

Another Passion

THE OTHER SPORT, apart from rugby, about which I am deeply passionate is golf. Being born and brought up in Scotland, where golf courses are usually close and accessible, even to children, I remember the times when I caught the bus down to Gullane Golf Club, on the east coast near to Muirfield, or sometimes up to the Braid Hills Golf Course in Edinburgh. We used to play four or five times a week in the school summer holidays, from quite a young age, which was a good time to start. Golf is a sport that you can always pick up and play to a reasonable standard, especially if you were lucky to have managed enough practice and had the opportunity to learn the rudiments of the game at a tender age.

I have a seven handicap which has remained fairly constant, primarily because my rugby-playing activities have curtailed opportunities to get out on the golf course and practice. Nonetheless, I am hopeful that in the future, when I am not playing serious rugby and can devote myself more to golf, I will improve on that handicap. Many people are aware that I have always nurtured an ambition to play in the British Open. It is probably one that I will never achieve, but that does not mean that one should not set one's sights on such a feat. Even though you have what, to some people, appears an impossible goal, there is nothing wrong in dreaming of, or in aiming at, such a challenge. I believe that dreams can come true, but only if you work hard at them and discipline yourself to practise. Natural talent can only get you so far, but you get nowhere in any sport unless you knuckle down and practise

179

relentlessly, which I believe is the only route to the top.

Who knows? In a few years time perhaps, I might just be lucky enough to tee off as one of the amateurs in the Open Championship. I am not one of those people who set themselves an ambition and then abandon it the following week. I always want to work hard in order to achieve, for I am a great believer that if you set your goals high enough, even to the point of impossibility, you can often accomplish them, or at least enjoy the challenge of getting close.

One of the great things about being involved at a high level of your chosen sport, and enjoying a sort of celebrity status, is the opportunity to play golf with some of the top professionals from around the world in Pro Am events. I have been lucky enough to play with Hale Irwin, Ian Baker-Finch, Ian Woosnam, Sam Torrance and Sandy Lyle, to name but a few, and in 1994, prior to his winning the Benson and Hedges at St Mellion, I played with Europe's most popular golfer, Seve Ballesteros. Golf is a truly wonderful game and it is probably the only sport in the world that you can play with, and against, the very best professionals and have a proper game. You cannot do this in tennis, or snooker, or darts. You could not run against them, you could not ski against them, you could not realistically play rugby or soccer against them but, because of golf's brilliant handicapping system, you have a chance of playing and beating the professional. Surely, for a game which encompasses and embraces all boundaries of sex, age, race and religion, it is without equal and gives it that stature which causes it to be so popular all over the globe. I feel very privileged to have played on so many magnificent golf courses in Scotland and around the world, and with so many fine professionals and amateurs alike.

I have been very fortunate to have played with the likes of Sam Torrance and the other fine players I have already mentioned. I have had the opportunity to share experiences with great golfers from all over the world during my many different tours and excursions. I have been able to learn where they come from, about their different cultures and environments, and have got to know them and made many good friends due to such privileged opportunities.

Sam Torrance is like the local hero, the people's champion in Scotland, but if you transpose on to the bigger world stage, I suppose the person I admire most in world golf just now is Greg Norman. He is a great ambassador of that world of golf, and he strikes me as being a true gentleman as well. He has overcome many disappointments in his life, and he came back majestically to win the British Open in the summer of 1993 in a manner that showed the character and the hallmark of the man himself. He is extremely popular among his peers and, as with all sports, I think the greatest thing that a fellow player can say about you is that he respects you. If they have respect for you as a sportsman and as a gentleman, then that is the greatest compliment that can ever be paid to you.

If there was one course on which I would happily play golf every day for the rest of my life, it would have to be the Old Course at St Andrews. There are a number of reasons, not least of which is playing the 17th and 18th holes, and driving off the 17th tee, over the railway sheds as they once were, though now they are modern-day buildings attached to the Old Course hotel. Coming up the 18th at St Andrews, a view that seems unchanged throughout history, and realising that you are striding down the same fairway as the greatest names in world golf, is a tremendous thrill. The adrenalin always surges when you play the 18th, for it is surely one of the most enchanting places on earth to play golf.

The opportunity for so many golfers from around the world to play on that course is a tribute to the way that the game transcends all boundaries. You look at other sports and, unless you are a top player, you would never get near, say Murrayfield, to play rugby, or Wimbledon to play tennis, or Wembley to play soccer, or Augusta to play golf; and yet you are able to play golf at St Andrews, on what is traditionally the most famous course of them all. Those who have played the Old Course will always remember the experience.

Rugby people often talk about those players alongside whom they would have liked to have played; but I would like to list 15 rugby players to play golf, matching their playing positions and the hole number. It would be a marvellous thing to do, to play with men that you admire most and for whom you have the utmost respect. Hopefully, you could also get some of your own back, as, for instance, Scotland have never beaten the All Blacks in rugby – we would have a very good chance of beating them on the golf course, and I would certainly be taking that match as seriously as any rugby Test.

Selecting those I would like to play golf with has been an interesting exercise, because they have had to be men to whom I related as personalities and players, both on and off the field, whether they were team-mates or opponents. These would be the men that I have respected the most during my lifetime in rugby football. My caddy would be Geech, because there is no man in rugby for whom I have greater admiration, and he may as well carry my clubs in the way that he has carried me and Scotland and the Lions around all the rugby grounds of the world.

I start off at the first hole with the finest number one to have played for Scotland, David Sole. He encompasses everything that is good about Scottish rugby. His aggression, commitment, dedication and discipline are without equal, which is why I accord him so much respect as a player and as a man. He is a keen and terrifying competitor, and nothing ever gives David the idea that he could not win a game. It was a shame that he retired, too early in my opinion, but I can understand the reasons, for he has a good job with United Distillers, a lovely wife, Jane, and now three splendid kids to look after. He certainly needs to work hard to make sure that his family are brought up in the way that he was, and I know that he wants only the best for them. Unfortunately, the stark reality is that he was not getting paid a penny to play rugby at International level and, if he was losing out on progressing in his job because of the dedication and discipline that he needed to apply to rugby, then you have to sympathise with his point of view. The loss of someone like David Sole was immeasurable to the Scottish pack, and I do not believe he has been adequately replaced. As to the golf, I would feel obliged to give David a shot, which, if used wisely, would secure him the half that his expectation would demand.

Next, I need to select a hooker for the second hole and I would choose Phil Kearns, the Australian captain, with whom I went on tour as part of the 1992 World XV to New Zealand. Phil is a big, brash and really nice guy, as well as being a mighty player. I do not think he would fit into any other country as easily as Australia, for the brashness and easy-going life suits his style and he is a very, very good guy to be on tour with. He is funny, he is committed and a hell of a rugby player, a tireless competitor on the field and a person who is a real star of the future. I would say that he is the epitome of the modern-day rugby player and I respect him enormously. I do not think Phil's golf would be up to much, so I would have to give him at least a couple of shots at this hole for him to have a chance of a half.

The tight-head prop that I would choose to play hole number three with is Jason Leonard, one of the great characters of modern-day rugby. Before people remind me that Jason is the loosehead prop for England, I am aware of the fact, but this did not stop him from switching sides during the Lions Tour to New Zealand. He is also too good a guy not to have in your side, and also too good a tourist not to take with you anywhere, and he therefore wins his place in this World XV from all sides. Jason is enormously strong and pushes weights like others push papers round their desks. He is a committed and disciplined forward, but he also knows how to relax in the traditional manner of rugby players. His golf will be rubbish, but his chat will be good, so he can take as many shots as he likes to get a half at this hole.

The fourth hole would be played with Ian Jones of New Zealand, the outstanding lock of the 1992 NZRFU's Centenary Series against the World XV, when, having damaged his collar bone in the first Test, he remained on the field and played in two more Tests, all within the space of eight days. He was the player of the series, carrying the New Zealand lineout on his own, winning everything. He is a tremendously agile and fluid player into the bargain. He is one of the new breed of rugby players, a modern All Black who manages to smile more than occasionally. He is quiet and diffident off the field, not the hard, raw granite of some of the old school New Zealand forwards, like Brian Lochore or Colin Meads and the rest, who were described by one of their own journalists in a book title as 'The Unsmiling Giants'. No doubt Ian is probably a half-decent golfer and therefore a shot given by me would secure his half.

I would play the fifth hole with another All Black second row, Gary Whetton, with whom I played in South Africa in October 1993, in a testimonial match for Naas Botha. Away from New Zealand and the intensity of the All Blacks, here is another super bloke, a very genuine guy and one hell of a competitor. He was dropped long before his time, as he showed in beating Grenoble and being man of the match for Castres in the 1993 French Cup final. He won so many Tests for the All Blacks with his tremendous athleticism in the line-out, where at his peak he was the world's best, and also in the loose, where he could run like a stag and handle like a fly half. He was a very big man with fine hands, great strength and athletic jumping ability to go with his general conviviality off the field. Such is his determination, he would probably call a half at this hole without the need for a shot to be given.

At hole number six, I would choose another real competitor

with whom I was on the Lions tour, Ben Clarke. For him to go out to New Zealand from England with the Lions and dominate as he did in 1993, to become one of their players of the year, was a tremendous achievement and worthy of his play. He has a tremendous future in the game and I have the greatest of respect for him as a rugby player. He is a marvellous tourist, great fun to be with and, again, a modern player, because he is such an athletic and dedicated forward. He is the sort of man that any young player should aspire to emulate. However, I know that he would need at least a couple of shots in order to get a half because golf is certainly too slow a game for Ben.

Hole number seven would be contested with Michael Jones of New Zealand, who is one of the most awesome rugby players that I have ever seen. Samoan by extraction and a deeply religious man, his principles do not allow him to play on a Sunday, which was one of the reasons why the All Blacks folded so easily against Australia in the semi-final of the World Cup, held on a Sunday in Catholic Dublin. Physically strong, extremely fast and an explosive player, he was at the peak of his powers in 1987 when he was a key figure in the All Blacks team which won the World Cup. He has overcome some terrible injuries, sustained because of the pace at which he played the game. He is still one of the best open-side wing forwards in the world. He is quiet and unassuming, a very popular All Black and a tremendous ambassador of his sport and for New Zealand. Michael is bound to be good at golf, because it would be a shame if he was not, but a shot would earn him his half too.

I would play the eighth hole with Tim Gavin, who is a rugged Australian of farming stock from the outback, who has moved into the city to concentrate on playing top-class rugby. He has tremendous athletic ability and is a hard, hard man in every sense of the word. I remember him destroying the England team in 1991, playing for New South Wales and Australia. His raw strength was quite extraordinary, and heaven knows what he is like hitting a golf ball. I have a feeling the ball would go a long way and, again, he is such a tremendous rugby player and competitor that one shot would see the hole being halved.

You always need a cheeky chappie in any rugby team, and there is no question in my mind that the cheekiest of them all is Gary Armstrong, a great scrum half and my partner for the ninth hole. I think that if Gary played rugby for any country other than Scotland he would be the most important sportsman in that country.

His immeasurable strength, his iron will, his spirit and example, not to mention his dedication and commitment, are an inspiration to everybody in the Scottish team. Yet he is entirely down to earth, unassuming, his own man, totally laid back and very mischievous. To give you an example, he will rush into your hotel room when you are not watching and steal the remote control, so that you are unable to change channels on the television. Someone may be running a bath and he will distract their attention, while at the same time putting a packet of hot chocolate powder into the bath, so that it all froths up into a brown mess. In any rugby team you need these off-the-field, lighter moments, to give the balance between such fun and the pressure of tuning in and preparing for a big game. Gary Armstrong can certainly provide that. He is another wonderful example to youngsters in the way that the game should be approached and played. In 1993, he declared himself unavailable for International rugby so that he could devote more time to his family. It took massive persuasion to bring him back into the Scottish side in 1994. However, his golf is erratic to say the least, and so no doubt he would need a few shots to earn his half.

At hole number ten you need a master controller, and one of the great virtuoso stand offs during my lifetime has been Michael Lynagh. He is the antithesis of the brash Australian, being a quiet, unassuming man, but fiercely competitive and a tremendous ambassador for Australian rugby. He kicks goals from all over the place, he is always as darting and slippery as a trout and one of the most elusive runners from stand off. He has a wonderful pair of hands and I would love to see him playing outside half to Gary Armstrong, which would surely be an unbeatable combination. He is a great kicker and passer of the ball and altogether a wonderful all-round player, who, in the summer of 1994 against Ireland, became the first man to score 800 points in Test matches. His golf is probably equally as good, and he would earn a half without a shot being given.

The 11th hole would be one of the most competitive, because I would really want to beat this guy on the golf course, knowing that I am not capable of beating him on the rugby field, for his name is David Campese. A free spirit if ever there was one, and rugby needs men like him. He is controversial, but he is so good, and that is a classic combination. If he says that he is going to do something, then the chances are that he will accomplish it. Above all, he is a craftsman and an artist, and it is the way that every rugby player in the world should wish to be, a true exhibitor of astonishing talents with an amazing sense of adventure. During the last World Cup he fought a personal crusade to ensure that Australia won it, and nobody could ever forget that second try in the semi-final against New Zealand, which was sheer genius. Running at speed on to a delicate probing kick by Lynagh, David feinted out and then inside the All Black defence before throwing an outrageous pass over his head, without looking, to Tim Horan, who scored to make it 13–0, thus burying the All Blacks. I would like to believe that on the golf course it would be a different matter and that I could produce one of my birdies to ensure that Campo would need to take a shot to earn him his half.

Jeremy Guscott would be my choice for the 12th hole, as he is one of the most subtle and silky smooth runners ever to grace the game. Jeremy is a hard man to get to know but if you accept that is the way he is, slightly shy and withdrawn at first, then I think one is able to get on with him and communicate with him, as I feel I have done. I do not suppose that he will ever be my best pal, but I respect him enormously as a rugby player and I like to think that he feels the same about me. He is not a bad golfer either but, again, I get very keen when I am playing against these three-quarters, because I know that I can compete with them on the golf course sometimes better than on the rugby field and therefore have a better chance of beating them at golf than in the open spaces of a rugby pitch. So, Jeremy, I am afraid you will need to take a shot to halve this one with me.

Without question, I choose Tim Horan for hole number 13. He is an all action rugby player, a bit like Gary Armstrong in build – stocky, with supreme strength, particularly in the upper body. He has tremendous speed off the mark, he appears to love contact, as shown by his aggressive tackling, and he has been a major factor in Bob Dwyer's midfield swarm defence. He has an undying commitment to winning any game for Australia and has an iron will in that regard, as well as being a tremendously good bloke, which all contributes to making him the best centre in the world at the moment. However, his golf cannot possibly be as good as his rugby, and he will need a shot at least for his half.

On the homeward stretch, it is good to meet up with my old pal, Ieuan Evans, at the 14th. Ieuan is a wonderful example of the wizardry of Welsh rugby, twinkletoes himself, a lovely guy, a great friend and magnificent tourist. He is not known to be over-emotional, which they say is a Welsh trait; he just gets on with his job with the minimum of fuss and that is what I like about him. I have great admiration for him and hold him in much esteem for the abilities he showed when on tour with the Lions. He is very easy to get on with and is hugely respected by his peers in International rugby. He is another wonderful example for youngsters to emulate and I believe he is one of the truly great contemporary rugby players, as he showed by his performances on the 1993 Lions tour, following his success in 1989 in Australia. Ieuan is the finest exponent of making tries out of nothing and he is never averse to stealing one from right under your nose, so I have a sneaking feeling that he might hole a long putt from across the green to earn his half.

The one full back on the 15th hole that I would like to play golf with is Roger Gould of Australia, because he was the first full back I really admired and identified with, in terms of my build and my philosophies on the game. He was never the quickest of players, but he had enormous strength and a kick like a mule. I once played against Roger in the Singapore Sevens and I keep bumping into him in Hong Kong. We always enjoy sharing a couple of lagers or whatever, and we like to chew the cud concerning rugby football and everything else. Roger is a smashing guy, very modest, and during his time as the Australian full back he really was the rock on which Australia, at that time, was founded. He played, of course, in the 1984 Wallaby Grand Slam side, which was one of the great teams, alongside Andrew Slack, the young David Campese and Michael Lynagh, and with Nick Farr-Jones and Mark Ella at half back. Roger was a player who made everything happen around him, by coming into the line, standing up big in the tackles, being totally secure in defence and kicking so beautifully. I have long admired him as the embodiment of the all-round full back and, because I modelled myself on him, I am desperate to get another birdie to ensure that Roger will require at least one shot for the half.

I have played 15 holes with the players that I would nominate as the best World XV that have played during my career. It is a highly personal choice and I am aware of the many other great players who would represent other people's preferences. You have to consider men like Serge Blanco, Phillippe Sella, Rory Underwood, Rob Andrew, Peter Winterbottom, Dean Richards, Grant Fox, John Kirwan, Sean Fitzpatrick, Finlay Calder and John Jeffrey, to mention but a few.

Having named my World XV, I can continue to enjoy and

amuse myself over the last three holes. Therefore, I would like to take with me the three teams who have given me some of the greatest pleasures of my life, over the closing holes. On the 16th I would like to have the Scottish team, all those tremendous men that I have played with, to enjoy the walk down the fairway, remembering old times, the tours we have been on, the games we won, or should have won, the tackles we put in and the tries that were scored, and the laughs that we had. That would be a great experience and we would all play the hole and go off together to be happy men, late into the night.

On the 17th hole I would want to take the British Lions players whom I have played with. The highest honour that any rugby player can achieve in these Isles is to play for the Lions, for there is something magical and mystical about them. The fact that they now only go on tour once every four years adds to the honour and to the drama and sense of occasion, and may that always be so. It would be very similar to the walk down the 16th, perhaps less intimate, for the Scottish team are like a family, but this would be compensated for by the quality of those who represent the British Isles, and I can assure you that they are all men worth the knowing.

Lastly, we come to the 18th hole and, bearing in mind that we will be going into the club house to have a few drinks at the 19th, I would want to play it with my family. My Mum and Dad, Isobel and Clifford, my brothers Graeme and Scott and their wives Jacqui and Jenny, younger brother Ewan, and, of course, last but certainly not least, my lovely wife Diane. I will take my family with me and pla the 18th hole and then go and enjoy a big family reunion, happy after playing a round of golf, and happy that I can look back on the unstinting support that I always had from them. We would rummage through all the fun times and all the wonderful memories that we have shared together, and the experiences that we have still to enjoy in this amazing world of rugby.

Within the teams that I have mentioned, I would have the utmost respect for each player, both on and off the field. They have earned it by their deeds on the pitch and by being gentlemen off it, and that is extremely important to me. It is one thing to be able to perform on the rugby field, but then you have to go on and look after the youngsters and be able to sell them the sport by interesting, encouraging, helping and educating them. Hopefully they will learn from you and have respect for you, by realising that, without your input, they themselves would not have been quite so good. That was the way it was for me, for it was by learning from and emulating men such as Donald Scott, John Rutherford, Roger Gould and many others, that I myself learnt to become a useful player.

Moving away from golf, many people have often asked, 'How are you going to cope after you have finished playing rugby? Won't you miss it desperately?' Yes, I will, but the important thing to realise is that there are other opportunities out there which must be grasped. I have already talked about reducing my golf handicap in an attempt to play in the British Open, which is a tremendous ambition to set. There are also other sports to learn and master, such as skiing, and although I have been lucky enough to ski in Vail, Colorado, and Jacksonville in Wyoming, the opportunities to do that when you are playing International rugby are very limited. So life after rugby will allow me to enjoy a different lifestyle. I have always been one to discipline and dedicate myself wholeheartedly to playing at the top level. I hope I will enjoy playing at a lower level, where the same dedication is not required. Much of these spare energies will undoubtedly be put into work, but I would also like to indulge in sports like squash and mountain biking, when I am not on the golf course.

One of the great advantages and pleasures that you get out of sport is that you meet so many people and, in some strange way, sporting participation seems to make communication easier. We are particularly lucky that we play rugby, which seems to give us a remarkable ability to mix with and enjoy the company of people from all walks of life, different backgrounds and different cultures and religions. Rugby transcends all these boundaries and I have been extremely fortunate and privileged to have played one of the great games of the world. All I can say is that it has been a hell of a lot of fun.

APPENDICES

Gavin Hastings' Record in Major Representative Matches

TEST APPEARANCES – SCOTLAND

				T	PG	C	DG*
1986	France	Murrayfield	18–17		6		
	Wales	Cardiff	15–22	1	1		
	England	Murrayfield	33– 6		5	3	
	Ireland	Dublin	10– 9		2		
	Romania	Bucharest	33–18		5	3	
1987	Ireland	Murrayfield	16–12			1	
	France	Paris	22–28		4	1	
	Wales	Murrayfield	21–15		2	2	
	England	Twickenham	12–21		2	1	
	France (RWC)	Christchurch	20–20		4		
	Zimbabwe (RWC)	Wellington	60–21	1		8	
	Romania (RWC)	Dunedin	55–28	2	1	8	
	New Zealand (RWC)	Christchurch	3–30		1		
1988	Ireland	Dublin	18–22		2	2	
	France	Murrayfield	23–12	1	4		
	Wales	Cardiff	20–25		4		
	England	Murrayfield	6– 9		2		
	Australia	Murrayfield	13–32	1	1	1	
1989	Fiji	Murrayfield	38–17	1	2	4	
	Romania	Murrayfield	32– 0		2	3	
1990	Ireland	Dublin	13–10				
	France	Murrayfield	21– 0		1		
	Wales	Cardiff	13– 9				
	England	Murrayfield	13– 7				
	New Zealand	Dunedin	16–31			2	
	New Zealand	Auckland	18–21		2	2	
	Argentina	Murrayfield	49– 3	1	1	5	

1991	France	Paris	9–15			
	Wales	Murrayfield	32–12		2	1
	England	Twickenham	12–21			
	Ireland	Murrayfield	28–25	1	1	
	Japan (RWC)	Murrayfield	47– 9	1	2	5
	Ireland (RWC)	Murrayfield	24–15		3	2
	Western Samoa (RWC)	Murrayfield	28– 6		4	2
	England (RWC)	Murrayfield	6– 9		2	
	New Zealand (RWC)	Cardiff	6–13		2	
1992	England	Murrayfield	7–25		1	
	Ireland	Dublin	18–10		2	2
	France	Murrayfield	10– 6		2	
	Wales	Cardiff	12–15		1	
	Australia	Sydney	12–27		2	1
1993	Ireland	Murrayfield	15– 3		1	1
	France	Paris	3–11		1	
	Wales	Murrayfield	20– 0		5	
	England	Twickenham	12–26		3	
	New Zealand	Murrayfield	15–51			
1994	Wales	Cardiff	6–29		2	
	England	Murrayfield	14–15		2	
	Ireland	Dublin	6– 6		2	
	France	Murrayfield	12–20		4	
	Played 50	**Points 454**		**10**	**98**	**60**

Test Appearances – British Isles

				T	PG	C	DG
1989	Australia	Sydney	12–30		2		
	Australia	Brisbane	19–12	1	1		
	Australia	Sydney	19–18		5		
1993	New Zealand	Christchurch	18–20		6		
	New Zealand	Wellington	20– 7		4		
	New Zealand	Auckland	13–30		2	1	
	Played 6	**Points 66**		**1**	**20**	**1**	

* *Abbreviations* T – try; PG – penalty goal; C – conversion; DG – drop goal

OTHER MAJOR REPRESENTATIVE MATCHES

Year	Match	Venue	Score	T	PG	C	DG
1986	Lions v Rest (IRB Centenary)	Cardiff	7–15		1		
1988	Barbarians v Australia	Cardiff	22–40	1			3
1989	Barbarians v New Zealand	Twickenham	10–21		2		
	Lions v France	Paris	29–27	2	4	1	
1990	Home Unions v Rest of Europe	Twickenham	43–18	1		1	6
1991	Scotland v Barbarians	Murrayfield	16–16				
1992	World XV v New Zealand	Christchurch	28–14		1		
	World XV v New Zealand	Wellington	26–54	1			
	World XV v New Zealand	Auckland	15–26				

MAJOR TOURS

Year	Tour		T	PG	C	DG
1985	Scotland to North America	played 4	4	4	2	
1987	World Cup		3	6	16	
1989	Lions to Australia	7	2	17	2	1
1990	Scotland to New Zealand	4		9	6	
1991	World Cup		1	13	9	
1992	Scotland to Australia	2		2	3	
1993	Lions to New Zealand		1	24	12	

OTHER INFORMATION

- **Cambridge Blues** – 1984, 1985
- **Scottish International Records**
  Most points in an International Championship Season – 52 in season 1985–86
- **Most points in Internationals**
  Twenty-seven points against Romania in 1987 set a new individual world record which lasted a few hours! Didier Camberabero scored 30 points against Zimbabwe later the same day.
- **The Teams**
  Has represented Watsonians, Cambridge University, London Scottish, Barbarians, Edinburgh, Anglo-Scots, Scotland and the British Isles.